De Vez en Cuando:
From Time to Time

Rick Johnson

De Vez en Cuando: From Time to Time
Copyright © 1996 by Rick Johnson

First Edition: January 1996
Second Edition: August   2002

Johnson, Richard (Rick) David
(Former title – The Making of a Missionary: De Vez en
Cuando: From Time to Time)
  De Vez en Cuando: From Time to Time
  I.   Christian Missions I. Title.
        ISBN 0-9648163-3-4

Published by
International Action Ministries
2610 Galveston Street
San Diego, CA 92110

All rights reserved. No part of this book may be
reproduced in any form or by any means whatsoever
without permission in writing from the author and
publisher.

Printed in Colombia

Dedication

I dedicate this book to my wife, Eunice, our parents, brothers, sisters and to my special friend, co-worker and brother in the faith, Jeff Huckabone.

It is also dedicated to the wonderful people with whom I have had the opportunity to work with all these years and the faithful, sacrificial partners who pray, encourage, support and make possible every aspect of this ministry.

Thank you for the greatest blessings in my life-- faith, hope and love.

Table of Contents

Introduction

A most compelling story in the Bible is the testimony of the blind man who admits, "I don't know much about who healed me or how He did it; but this I am positive about, I was blind and now I see." Nothing is more powerful than the personal testimony of someone that God has changed.

Rick honestly and realistically tells his personal journey through disease, danger and challenges of being a missionary. This book is humorous yet very serious and makes us take a second look at our traditional Christian assumptions. We need to take another look at the values and assumptions that have been guiding our methods in Christian missionary work. This book will take you to that new perspective.

Rick's story leads to conclusions that I share. He and I also share a passion for the hurting and the lost that can be your passion as well. His vision of seeing those who are today's "ministry" being equipped to be tomorrow's "ministers," reflects my own vision from working for the Waodani (also known as "Aucas") who speared my father to death in the Ecuadorian jungles in 1956.

Rick's book gives insight, inspiration and hope for ordinary men and women who desire to be used by God.

Steve Saint
I-TEC Missionary, Ecuador

We who call ourselves "Christ's disciples" need to be shaken up from time to time (de vez en cuando). It's far too easy to measure ourselves by what's considered "normal Christianity" all around us and to come out feeling okay. What we really need is to look away from the mainstream of Christianity, and to take a fresh and brutally honest look at Jesus Himself, and what He has called us to. Rick's story is an opportunity to do just that. His life and story is both a blessing and a bother and it's just what we need!

Rick is asking the right questions about the discrepancy between clear biblical priorities and the things which make up our actual pursuits in life. He humbly admits that we are forever falling short, but this is no reason to give up our pursuit of Christ!

This book is not about challenging everyone to "get involved in missions"; it's much more fundamental than that. This book is about presenting our lives to God for His use, however and wherever He sees fit, here and now. It's about asking the hard questions regarding discipleship where the rubber meets the road. In Rick's case, this led to missionary labor. In your case, it may lead to something entirely different. Let's follow Rick's example of giving our lives to Christ, and enjoy the adventure of becoming active participants in God's plan.

Ron VanPeursem
New Tribes Mission, Executive Committee

Unlike most people who have met Rick, I have only known him on the jungle end of his adventures, here among the Yanowamo Indians who for many years have stirred his passions and sharpened his focus on seeing the Kingdom of God established in all the world.

His visits to our area have always been cause for excitement among missionaries and Indians alike; and I have long appreciated his total commitment to giving himself to those he serves, sharing even the darkest and most difficult moments of their lives and struggles. But even more, I treasure the moments we shared and discussed what it really means to belong to Christ, to know Him and to make Him known.

I'm glad those same concepts that encouraged and challenged us in our primitive settings here, are now available for a wider audience, through these pages. You'll find in them a call to examine your faith, and your commitment; and to abandon the comfort of just going with the flow, in Christian circles. It's a message that is greatly needed, and I pray it will be used of God in a mighty way. Thank you, Lord, for Rick and Eunie.

Marg Jank
New Tribes Mission missionary

One of the most compelling reasons to read this book is because of the things this book is not. It's not a quick fix, five-step, prepackaged hard-sell approach to missions. Rather it is a book that seeks to honestly work through some of the fundamental issues associated with growing and maturing in your Christian life.

In fact, you may find that this book actually causes you to ask more questions than it answers.

On a personal note, the Scripture says, "*A man of many friends comes to ruin, but there is a friend who sticks closer than a brother,*" in Proverb 18:24. Rick has been this kind of friend to me over the past 25 years and for that I am extremely blessed.

It has been a unique privilege on numerous occasions to confess to people when asked, that yes, I am "that Jeff" in Rick's book.

Jeff Huckabone
President, TEAM Manufacturing Inc.

Here is a book which is, above all, honest. It is a heart rendering series of real Christian adventures. How could such a young man go through so much and still live; it defies all reason.

As his pastor for many years, I encouraged Rick to get formal Bible training, but he chose not to. Maybe it would have distracted him and kept him from learning from the Master Teacher Himself.

If you don't want to be challenged, please don't read this book. If you want a tonic for your soul, read this book and pass it on to a friend.

Rick has found the secret to God's heart by loving and helping the poor and outcast of this world. *"He who gives to the poor lends to the Lord."*

God has given Rick a wonderful wife, Eunie. What a gift from God. A lady who has the same heart for God and His people.

This is a book that is difficult to put down until you're finished reading it.

Ray Hahn
Pastor Emeritus
Clairemont Emmanuel Church
San Diego, California

Rick tells in his book of experiences from almost 25 years ago in the Amazon. There he first met my parents and then later me. My family's friendship with Rick after all these years continues to be a taste of what our fellowship in heaven is going to be.

Rick has always shown much compassion and love for people. I have observed him with the Yanomamö, who affectionately call him "Yanomamö Blushishiwä" ("white Yanomamö"); I saw this same dedication and compassion years ago when we visited him and his work in Mexico.

As you read Rick's book, an optimistic attitude is echoed through his writing, yet in his narrative, he takes us not only through the heights of serving God, but also relates the heart break, discouragement and despair many times known but seldom told by missionaries.

This is not a book that you can read and forget. It will challenge your views on missions and missionaries.

Mike Dawson
Yielded Evangelical Servants Missionary

Unlike most Christians I know, Rick likes to keep his teachings simple. Whenever I am around him, I think about when Jesus' disciples asked him why he used parables to talk to the people and Jesus replied, "The knowledge of the secrets of the Kingdom of God has been given to you, but to the rest it comes by means of parables, so that they may look but not see and listen but not understand."

Rick can see and understand things that many other missionaries who have come to Mexico to work with underprivileged people cannot see or understand. Rick respects and treats every person equal regardless of their economic and social circumstances or level of education. The way he presents the Gospel to our people is not only simple, attractive and comprehensive but he delivers his message to us in our own words and perspectives. He has the gift of becoming one of us.

As much as he is simple, he is profound. Every one of his experiences in this book is filled with profound teachings, but presented in a simple way that will be enjoyed by all. You won't want to miss them.

Oscar Escalada
CEO, Mexican Federation of YMCAs

Preface

De vez en cuando, in English: From time to time. We reflect and take time to look back, from time to time. Life's short span should not allow for many such stops, yet, from time to time, we all look back to remember, to meditate and to consider. As we do, we reflect on faces, experiences, places and events which have formed and altered our being, our values, our perspective and our purposes in life.

The following story is not one reflecting the events and changes or accomplishments of any number of men, but rather a collection of events reflecting an onward moving process of the Spirit of God, being hindered by sin and many shortcomings.

It is an incomplete story touching on those things which reflect real and true Christianity in contrast to that which is perceived as real Christianity. Although in no way is this small collection of reflections and events meant to be a final authority on any specific issue, these events are bits of history that have greatly affected my convictions and perceptions.

The story would be much more complete if not for the sin nature in my life which has from the beginning slowed and hindered the best from coming to maturity. Still, day after day, this same nature battles against the Spirit of God affecting aspects of my life and work. I must be the first to admit that man truly does not learn from his mistakes, for although I fall short countless times,

I return to fall again. For any good that can be extracted from these pages, the glory must be given to Him who produced the good, Jesus Christ.

This collection of events, perspectives and history grew from my earlier writings, as well as tapes, journal entries, notes, testimonies and other recorded accounts from over the years. They are personal and not meant to be "authority" for any other's life.

Every one of our lives is a puzzle slowly being assembled. Each experience, person and place is represented among the literal millions of pieces making each of us who we are. These collective pieces of our life's puzzle reflect who we are through our attitudes, convictions, actions and faith.

Rick Johnson

1
Growing Up in a Dead Church

I was born in North Carolina on July 16, 1961; a year later we moved to San Diego, California.

Both my parents came from strong Christian homes. I give thanks to God for having been raised in a Christian family with a very special younger sister. My parents loved us very much.

Sundays we would go to church together. I grew up in church. Church was what Sunday was all about. Every Sunday was basically the same: wake up, eat together as a family, get dressed for church. Always a last minute fight as one of us would hold up the works as we were ready to pile into the station wagon and head for church. An eternal struggle with Mom and Dad was a part of each Sunday service. There never seemed to be sufficient registration cards in the back of the pew on which to draw or scribble. The sermons were long and boring; we kids could in no way sit still. Church was a drag, the last place any kid would want to spend half his weekend.

In those early preteen years, I was a terror to my parents and the poor volunteer Sunday school teacher; in fact I think she was no more excited about Sunday school than I was.

Upon arrival at the church, my sister and I would quit pulling each other's hair and fighting and would depart, in peace, each to our own Sunday school class. I was fifty percent of my class. Jay was the other. Together we suffered through this weekly ritual. The most excitement in going to Sunday School was at the close when we received our weekly Christian comic book.

After class, we would proceed outdoors to break off pieces of church plants and throw them at other kids until church started or we got into trouble. My parents certainly couldn't have expected me to really get anything out of the sermon. In fact, I don't know how much of it even meant anything to them. As far as any of us knew, this was about all you could expect, and if you were to be Christian you had to go to church. Although I drew a thousand stick men and race cars on the back of registration cards and slept through as much of the "sit down" part of the service as possible, some of that "Jesus stuff" somehow still made it into my mind. I gathered early that understanding the sermon wasn't as important as just being in church. You just had to be in church. Oh, and not bother anyone else during church as Mr. B did when he yelled out one morning during the sermon for someone to run. He had one of those small radios in his pocket with an earphone in his ear to hear the baseball game; I guess he forgot he was in church.

At eleven years old, I went to Christian camp. Camp was different from church. At camp we had a good time, and when they preached at us, we could kind of understand what they wanted. One night, I guess the Lord had enough of my nonsense. I had been fighting with another boy at the camp, and when it came time for the evening meeting, I went planning with some other guys to finish off the fellow camper. The plans fell by the wayside, however, when we saw that there would be more than just a preacher yelling at us. They had one of those flannel graph things. An old lady went up and started flopping flannel here and there and talking up a storm at the same time. I don't remember how she started off but it was something about heaven and hell.

On one side of the flannel graph she had the world which she identified as where we were. On the other side, she threw up some nice castle and said it represented heaven. Between the two, she plastered some red felt that looked like fire and told us it was hell; the more red felt she threw on, the hotter it got. You know the rest of the story. She finally put a cross over the fire then they had a prayer. She asked for those of us who wanted to be saved out of that fire to raise our hands. Mine went straight up. Flannel or no flannel, I didn't like the way that old lady said I was going to burn.

You can imagine the big change that came about in my life that night. After a special counseling time and prayer, those of us who, as they said, "accepted God," were given a certificate, dated and signed, confirming our "salvation." I went home a changed boy, until the camp high wore off. Then it was back to throwing rocks at the other kids at church, fighting with my sister and just being my old self. About a year later, my sister's Sunday school class membership had become even less successful than my class of two. With only one left in her class, the teacher quit and my parents were forced to set out in search of another church that would keep us kids out of trouble and from falling away from the most important thing, going to church. I didn't want to change churches. Although I didn't like our old church, I certainly did not want to go to another church where I knew no one.

A number of weeks later, we had chosen a new church. Although only twelve years of age, I noticed many differences between the new church and the church from which we had come. At the old church the emphasis was on being quiet and not running in the hallway, not playing around and keeping our clothes clean. The minister always dressed up like God. He wore a fancy bathrobe and always talked in a low voice. He even kind of looked like God as he sat on his big throne chair or preached behind that big wooden box. The adults called it a "pulpit." That sounded spiritual enough, so we never questioned why the pastor had to stand behind it to talk about God. You only saw him on Sunday, and he always patted me on my head as if I were a little dog when we walked out the door after church was over. I was always too young to say what all the adults had to say as they walked by the minister. "That was a very nice sermon, Reverend," or "Oh Reverend, what a beautiful message." I was always just glad to get out of there and throw a few rocks at the little kids. I hated church.

This new church was real strange. I guess the old people's meetings were kind of the same except people didn't seem to get so uptight about us kids making noise during the sermon and the preacher didn't dress in funny clothes. He even shook my hand at the door instead of patting me on the head. What shocked me more, though, was that the youth group was considerably larger than that of the other church. Instead of just two of us for Sunday school, this new church had hundreds of youth coming out. Instead of hearing some boring story in old English that even the Sunday School teacher had trouble reading, they used a Bible that spoke our kind of talk and the youth minister sounded as though he was really excited about the Bible. We even sang songs that I liked singing. Some guys played guitars and pianos instead of that haunted-house organ music we had at the other church. I had never seen this before. I didn't think anyone could be really excited about church.

Wednesday was even wilder. More than 400 youth came to hear the youth pastor speak. Many rode bikes and skateboards to church and didn't even get screamed at for having them inside. Everyone wore tennis shoes, jeans and shorts. Even bathing suits were okay and the youth pastor dressed like a real person also. He was excited about the Bible and didn't hide behind a pulpit box to talk. He sat on an old stool surrounded by all us kids sitting on the floor. You could even lie down and no one cared.

I had heard some of the Bible stories he was telling, but he told them like they really happened, not like something out of some dusty old story book. This youth pastor's name wasn't Reverend or Minister; everyone just called him Von. I never really had any of this new stuff figured out, but for the first time I looked forward to going to church, and I liked hearing the Bible stories. Von was kind of strange. You could visit him during the week. He was always doing things with the kids. His day off was Thursday, but it didn't really seem like a day off. Thursdays he would leave early for Mexico and not return until late. He had a "side ministry" there.

When I was almost thirteen, something happened that I'll never forget. It was one Wednesday night. After Von finished his Bible study, he came up to me and asked, "Hey, why don't you go down to Mexico sometime with me? I'm going tomorrow." At the age of twelve, I was fairly quick to remember that Thursday was a school day and that this could present itself as a great opportunity to get out of school, mess around all day, eat tacos, see the crazy driving in Mexico and play around with the orphan kids whom Von visited each week. I waited anxiously for my loving mom to pick me up after the meeting. I'll never forget the moment she pulled up.

"Mom, you won't believe it. Von asked me if there is any way possible for me to go help him work in Mexico tomorrow. He really needs help bad, and I don't want to let him down."

Mom was either overwhelmed that I was anxious to do anything extra that was church related or she felt bad that Von was so desperate for help that he had asked me to go with him. Anyway, she worked it out to get me excused from school and I was off. I took my "straight" face off as soon as she dropped me off at church to meet the Mexico work team. I was ready, ready to play, mess around and cause trouble!

2
Jeff and Joy Rides for the Elderly

It was some time after noon when I got tired of playing around and walked into the orphanage to check out what Von was doing. I was shocked. Here was the guy that took the place of the reverend, the guy that you wouldn't imagine as someone who could get dirty or really work, my pastor? There he was on his knees in a puddle of water washing kids' feet! Although the whole impact did not hit me at that moment, it was made. Here, all those Bible stories, all the things I had heard about Jesus being good and helping others, someone was actually doing it, actually living the words of the Bible, not just preaching them. This was something I had never even heard of before.

These first experiences were Biblical, to say the least, and were part of what laid a non-hypocritical foundation for me to really see the Word as something applicable to the real world outside, not just something to be listened to inside the church.

As I continued to mature, I became involved in some of the other activities sponsored by the youth group. Sunday afternoons Von took us to the old folks' home to visit and then to the children's ward to walk extremely physically and mentally handicapped kids around the block in their wheelchairs. We worked in Mexico, went to help people on the street and visited nursing homes. Those years held many experiences which in later years were to help mold some strong convictions. In time, I would be exposed to other kinds of youth ministry with different emphases and goals. But, for that time, Von helped us to focus on understanding God's love and putting it into practice. In later years, I saw other youth ministers and ministries that focused on fellowship, fun and growing a big group. Most of us who went through Von's teaching didn't sense any real purpose or fun in such self-centered activities.

Though changes were coming about in Von's original program, he continued to challenge all of us who were in his group to ask probing questions. What about our faith? What does the Bible really teach? Does God want us, His followers, to actually get involved? There was a constant challenge to look out beyond our own little worlds.

About age fifteen, I had become good friends with a brother in the Lord who was as much a troublemaker as I. Jeff and I spent much time together visiting in the old folks' homes and even playing jokes from time to time on some of the people we knew there.   Jeff liked setting one particular lady's alarm clock to go off at 3:00 a.m. The lady to this day, though, still loves us both!

In one of the convalescent homes, the food was terrible. The people who worked there were not very nice to the residents. There were strict rules which made life sad for our friends. Jeff and I would sneak pastries into the institution and have parties with our elderly friends there.

Later I bought a real fast car. A few times Jeff and I took the residents on "joy rides." Oh how they enjoyed the loud engine, burning tires and scary tours! They really appreciated the smuggled treats and loved the wild rides. They enjoyed all of our misguided attempts to add some spice to their lives. We would sing and pray with different ones there, but it seemed their eyes would sparkle most when we had some mischief planned. They always asked for more.

Jeff and I spent a lot of time discussing all this Christianity life-style stuff and after much time came to questions that would prove to be difficult ones to answer. If in fact it is God's will that all men have the opportunity to hear His Word, understand His love and salvation and come to a knowledge of the truth, then what should be our response to knowledge about people groups that have yet to hear His Word and have no way of calling on the name of Jesus for their salvation?

Certainly, if it were God's priority for all men to know Him, it seemed to make sense that it should be our priority as well. And so the considerations, prayers and questions began. In early 1979, at the age of seventeen, we had decided to go to the mission field and see for ourselves what this work was really all about. This was before the flood of the many short-term organizations that were to come offering summer projects on overseas fields.

We had heard lots of stories about hidden tribal groups in the Amazon of South America. Neither Jeff nor I realized how much these people would become part of our lives.

Within my mind, the thick, green Amazon territory was both a reality and a dream. The sobering reality: primitive tribal groups still wandering through the rain forests with little or no knowledge that another world existed outside their jungle canopy. They had no knowledge that a God exists who wants to call them out of their fear, witchcraft, endless warfare and avenging deaths caused by what they believe to be curses carried out by evil spirits. That was the reality. The dream: that these people would become a very real part of my life, that I would come to know them and understand them, their lives and the world in which they live.

Von

3

Rick & Jeff's Professional Landscape Company

It was a warm spring day when I called Jeff.

"Jeff, I've got a great idea how we can earn money for our trip." Twenty minutes later, Jeff's excitement evaporated as we stood below a tall palm tree. As Jeff shook his head, I explained how we could tie a rope around the top of the tree and around our waists to keep from falling, while we trimmed the dead fronds which everyone seems to dislike so much. It took a little talking and encouraging for Jeff to try it. It was a little scary. Nevertheless, all things balanced out and on that day **Rick and Jeff's Professional Landscape Company** was born!

By the following weekend, our company was organized and offering its professional services to the public. Jeff was a step ahead of me arriving at the first door. We were scared but confident. May God forgive us. We really thought we were doing the right thing. God's patience is much more than many of us understand. There we were ready to earn our money for the mission field. God was with us; how could we go wrong? I guess we had a lot to learn about His ways, but at least our direction was on track.

The lady opened the door and we gave her our friendly greeting.

"Hi, we're from Rick and Jeff's Landscape Company. We are in your area this week only with a special on palm trees." I don't know many women who like seeing a "special" slip by, and this lady was no exception. It wasn't a half hour later we were hanging by two nylon ropes out of the top of her very tall palm tree. Needless to say, when she came out and saw us, it was obvious she had doubts about the credibility of our "professional" landscape enterprise. But Jeff was always quick to come up with an explanation for everything, including the reason we didn't have a truck to haul away the hundreds of cut palm fronds. We would tie them up for the trash man to haul away. What could she say? We were in her area one week only and with a "special."

As we continued our no-nonsense landscape business, we quickly learned secrets to earn even more cash. It was simple. We figured God would help us no matter what. After all, we were giving our lives to Him. We were going to the mission field!

Whenever anyone would ask, "Do you boys know how to...," we would cut them off in mid-sentence to quickly remind them, "Of course we know how; we are professionals. We do it all the time." I guess people wondered. With Jeff's old two-tone gray Volkswagen dune buggy, shovels and saws hanging out the windows, perhaps we didn't look too professional. But we sounded good, and we had "specials." For older people, we would do the work and leave without charging them if we felt it might be a hardship to them to pay. They thought it a bit strange after agreeing on a price and completing the job that we would tell them there is no charge and then drive off.

Business seemed to be picking up. We worked after school and Saturdays. One Saturday, we had quite a busy schedule and were in a hurry. We were finishing up another palm tree special when the lady came out to ask if we knew how to remove trees.

"Lady, of course we do. We're professionals. Don't you remember? We do it all the time." How could we pass up an opportunity? Jeff and I were in a hurry and we didn't have all of our "professional" tools with us (our tool collection amounted to two saws, rope, an ax, two shovels and two clippers). Because of the hurry, we decided it would be much easier to simply pull this small tree out with the car.

We quickly tied all our pieces of rope together which resulted in a single rope of sufficient length to reach from the bumper of the dune buggy, around the front corner of the house, through the gate, down the side of the house, around the back corner, and around the tree. We had struggled to pull plants out with the buggy before. This time we would avoid all the noise, smoking and spinning tires which usually went with wrestling trees from the ground. We would attempt to pull it out with one full-powered pull.

Jeff stood at the corner of the house to signal me, the driver of the company car, when to step on the gas. When he dropped his hand I started down the driveway, looking behind me to avoid running into a car in the street. I felt the rope tighten, but never realized that the tree had pulled out of the ground, roots and all, and had already slung around the back corner of the house like a rock out of a sling shot. I continued backing up, gaining speed. Jeff saw what was coming very quickly down the side of the house. The tree was flying parallel when it got to the fence and gate. Smash, the gate and fence were down. Jeff, to save his own life, had taken a dive out of the way.

It took a moment after seeing what had happened to regain our professional composure. We pulled the tree out of the way and were propping up the gate and fence; when, all of a sudden, the front door opened. As the lady walked out to the driveway, Jeff and I quickly leaned up against the gate and fence as if taking a rest. She stood smiling at us and in her hands she held two bowls of ice cream.

"How is it going, boys?"

We both answered, "Great. Things are going great." We were both a bit nervous standing ever so still holding the fence up. She just stood there looking at us and we just stood there looking at her.

"Well boys, how would you like some ice cream?" Jeff and I looked at each other with both amazement and fear. There was no way we were going to take our hands off that fence and cause the poor woman a heart attack seeing her fence fall over. On the other hand, she wasn't about to walk with her nice shoes through all the dirt that lay between us and the driveway.

She looked at us as if we were both crazy and asked again, "Boys would you like the ice cream?" This time she sounded a little harsh. She couldn't believe that we would just stand there.

We both answered, "Sure, we love ice cream; we would love to have the ice cream." Jeff looked at me to come up with some smart idea, but he saw that I was looking at him the same way.

Jeff finally spoke up, "We are just taking a short break over here by the fence. Why don't you just put the ice cream down on the ground and we will eat it when our rest is over."

Looking back, it really is amazing we didn't end up in jail! One day Jeff called me all excited about a big job he had landed. I was encouraged until he spilled the details. It was a citrus grove.

"No way!" I told him, "You really have to know what you're doing to prune fruit trees." I couldn't believe Jeff would be crazy enough to claim experience in something like professional care of fruit trees. Jeff got a bit upset with me and reminded me that we were indeed professionals and that everything would turn out fine. Besides, Jeff said, he had a magazine article explaining how to prune citrus trees.

I doubted the owners' confidence. We drove up in Jeff's ugly gray dune buggy and a rented U-Haul® truck. Jeff led the way with the chainsaw roaring, hacking wildly through the orange trees. One of the owners, an older lady, came out to check on us. She asked a few questions about how we were going about our work. I don't remember our answer, but it was clear that she had some major doubts about our qualifications. They had never seen any tree pruning like ours before!

I was sincerely worried about what the results of our mad hacking would be. When we were done, it looked like a hurricane had destroyed the grove. We hauled away all the damage in the truck, back and forth to the dump. I was worried! Jeff saw my worry as a joke. What if we had ruined the grove? We could be in real big trouble. Later the orchard owners did call us! They wanted to thank us as they had never had such a bumper crop before our servicing their grove! We were highly recommended again.

This was just one of many messes in which we seemed to find ourselves. Somehow, each time everything worked out great and most of our business ended up being referrals from our happy customers. The Rick and Jeff Professional Landscape Company continued.

4
Off to Venezuela

Neither my parents nor Jeff's were real excited about the idea of our going to the Amazon. They were much less impressed when they noted how little we knew about our trip.

"Where are you guys going?"

"We don't really know."

"Who are you going to work with?"

"We don't know."

"Who is going to pick you up down there?"

"We don't know."

"Who is in charge of this trip?"

"We are!"

"From whom do you have permission?"

"We have a letter that says, 'We will look forward to seeing you. Call this number and let us know when you will arrive.' "

We really didn't know a whole lot but we continued to pray over this burden on our hearts. God confirmed again and again that He in fact was leading us and we needed to keep our eyes on Him, to walk in faith. God tested our faith. In whom did we have our confidence? Various ones in our church began counseling us not to go.

"You might get sick. You would be better stewards of the funds if you stayed home and sent the funds to a missionary instead of going yourselves. You are too young. You don't have any training. You are getting sidetracked. Finish your education first. Get a Bible degree, then seminary and then start thinking about where you might work." Our heads were spinning with all the "counsel."

Our pastor, however, never moved. He never gave us any big spiritual lecture, but when we went to him to share our discouragements, he would simply encourage us to read the Word and ask the Lord about everything. Keeping in the Word together gave us our strong resolve and direction. Keeping in prayer together gave us more confidence and conviction. We continued on.

Though the discouragements were many, the conviction remained. There were questions as well. Why did so many have doubts about our trip, and why were counselors directing us away? We observed that not even one of our doubting brothers ever said that he prayed about the situation or that his considerations were a result of prayer and seeking God's direction through the Word. This was disturbing to us as young Christians. Although many had their doubts, Jeff and I remained tough, and, through our study and prayer, we remained steadfast.

We thought nothing could stand in our way, and nothing did. Our faith remained firm until the day before the deadline to purchase our plane tickets. Jeff and I sat in the car in front of his parent's house. Night had fallen and with it our spirit. We were praying.

God had not provided as we had expected. It was the last hour and Jeff, after putting together his last pennies, was $200 short. There was no one to turn to, no other resource and seemingly no hope. Before we prayed, Jeff and I discussed that it didn't seem possible that the Lord could have directed us this far just to have everything fall apart for a mere $200. In our confusion and frustration we prayed, "Lord, you brought us this far. Why don't we have all the money? You are going to look bad if you don't come through. We told everyone you were leading us this way. If you want us to go, you have to do something before tomorrow when we have to buy the tickets. It's in your hands. Amen."

Jeff got out of the car and walked toward his house; I started the car and drove toward home. I felt numb driving down the dark street not knowing what would happen. When I arrived at my parent's house, there was a message to call Jeff. I picked up the phone and called. Jeff answered but his voice now reflected something he had not had ten minutes earlier.

Jeff explained, "When I went into the house, I picked up my mail and went to my room. There was a letter from my grandmother who doesn't know about the trip. With the letter was a check for $200." Again, God showed us that it was in Him we needed to trust, not the approval of others or even our work or abilities to earn our way.

The day finally arrived. The last hours were filled with the final packing and preparations. At the airport there were plenty of doubts showing in everyone's eyes. Our parents, a few good friends and a number of others had come to see if we were really going to go through with it. We climbed the steps of the plane after our last good-byes. At the top of the steps we turned for one last look at our doubting friends. We walked through the door, down the aisle and sat silently in our seats. A bit quiet, not knowing what to expect. The plane took off into the dark night sky.

We felt a little disappointment to have been assigned seats next to an obnoxious old drunk, but we soon found that he was a friendly obnoxious drunk. He knew how to fend for himself and he extended his expertise to us also. After the stewardess served snack sandwiches to everyone and we had swallowed ours down, the drunken man leaned over, and with a twinkle in his eye asked, "How would you boys like some more?"

"Sure," we quickly answered back. We didn't know if there would be much food where we were going and we didn't have much money to be buying any extras, so we were very happy about the possibility of some more sandwiches. The drunken man started calling out to the stewardess and whistling at her. Jeff and I were not raised to be so impolite but we were pleasantly impressed at the effectiveness of this style.

"Hey, these boys want some more sandwiches. Bring 'em on." After they passed out blankets and turned off the lights, everything was quiet for a few minutes. But I guess it was too early for our new friend to sleep. He started to sing and whistle. It was quite some time before he finally got bored and went to sleep.

After flying through the night, we arrived in Miami, tired but in good spirits. We soon learned that from this point on we would have to be flexible. We would need to learn a bit about a culture foreign to us.

After picking up our suitcases from the luggage carrousel, we wandered around the airport until it was time to check in for our Caracas, Venezuela flight. At the check-in counter, we encountered a new type of "efficiency."

Most of the passengers were Venezuelan. They demonstrated a method of getting things done we had not seen before. We quickly fell behind. Those who lined up in orderly fashion only demonstrated their lack of interest to get on the flight. On the other hand, those who pushed the hardest and yelled the loudest at the ticket agent got the best service. Neither Jeff nor I were effective in this new method; we were one of the last to check in.

The flight left late in the evening. We had really no idea what we would encounter landing on the other end, so we did what we could to grab as many of those peanut snack bags from the stewardess as we could. At least we would have enough peanuts to survive the next day.

Still being quite unaware of the way things were, we missed out on the first part of a big round of applause after the plane landed. We weren't sure if everyone on the plane--almost all Venezuelan-- were clapping because they thought it was a good landing or if they were simply overjoyed that we made it without incident; for whichever reason, we joined in the last round of applause.

The stewardesses should have just given up trying to keep the passengers seated. A good three minutes before the plane ever got to the gate; most people had already stood up, grabbed their handbags and had headed to the door. We just laughed as the flight attendants tried to convince all the passengers that it was best to wait in their seats. We cleared customs with little trouble and then proceeded beyond the doors to a waiting gang of shoe shiners, luggage carriers and taxi drivers, everyone pulling us in a different direction.

5

Arrival in the Amazon

Finally, a friendly face showed up in the crowd, a real live missionary welcoming us to Caracas, Venezuela.

From this point on, it is important to remember that the experiences of these first months in the jungle were recorded by two young men who had no way of gauging accurately the experiences or dangers they encountered; neither had they any previous experience living in this new world.

We spent the night in an apartment the mission had in the big city. Although we were somewhat accustomed to the Spanish we heard so often in Mexico, we felt as though we were in an entirely different world. The customs were very different, and the Spanish spoken in Venezuela did not seem to resemble any of that we had heard before.

Early the next morning, we returned to the airport only to experience twice the chaos as the day before. We were very impressed with our new missionary friend who performed quite well in the routine of pushing and yelling. In a short time he had our tickets. One hour after taking off, we were landing in the frontier town of the Amazon territory. On approach, we watched the pilots through the open doors as they argued. One pilot pushed a couple levers; the other yelled at him and pulled the controls back. The arguing went on as did the changing of the plane controls. Jeff and I looked at each other in dismay as another humorous event unfolded.

Because the flight was so rough and the pilots seemed undecided as they made various changes in the plane's speed, direction and approach to the small landing field, both Jeff and I were encouraged that the plane landed without wrecking. We expressed our appreciation with the others with a long-lasting round of enthusiastic clapping.

As we left the plane we were met by some of the missionaries who work in the small town supplying the others working in the interior. Surrounded by dense jungle, the town had no roads leading in or out. Some cars, a good number of motorcycles and a few trucks were the extent of the town's traffic plus one flight each day from the city. Supplies were expensive and many times very limited as everything was brought in by plane or river barge; they seldom arrived on schedule. We parked ourselves in the humble but pleasant mission home. We hung our hammocks to avoid spots in the roof where the rain poured through. The next day we met the fellow whose home we would help build in the jungle.

After several days buying our supplies and preparing for living in the interior, we were taken to the airport. In a Cessna 185, we made our flight over the rugged jungle mountains. Our destination was inhabited by a small tribe of indigenous people living in the same manner they have for hundreds of years.

We flew into a secluded jungle airstrip next to a river where the missionary had sent ahead some supplies by boat. From there we would make shuttle flights into the village. The flight in the small mission plane was fairly smooth, although we missed the nice stewardess who was expected on most flights to bring us endless   bags   of peanuts,   cokes   and sandwiches. Jeff was let off at the first airstrip to load supplies; I went into the village to unload the supplies being airlifted in. The plane was only able to make two trips before   the   clouds   descended   into   the   valley making it impossible to continue flights that day.

It is difficult explaining those first impressions: the jungle, the tribal people surrounding us, watching everything we did. Their style of dress was a little different from ours, to say the least; a loin cloth for the men, a simple string tied around their waist for the women. We probably looked as interesting to them as they did to us.

Lack   of   understanding   about   my   new surroundings   in   the   jungle   made   for   some disheartening reflections for my daily journal. With Jeff in another village, I had no one with whom to discuss my perceptions. Perhaps I was afraid of things I didn't need to fear. Nonetheless, there I was trying to act cool as could be with this missionary whom I had barely met. I didn't want him to think I was just some stupid kid that would get in his way for the next two months. Although I know the jungle, after having spent a number of years collectively there, my first trip was limited to little real knowledge and the rest was, well, a combination of fear and trying to act cool.

It was late in the afternoon when one of the tribesmen came to talk to the missionary. He spoke a language unlike any I had ever heard. Unfortunately, the missionary had only been in this village a short time and did not really know the people's language either. Nevertheless, he got the message.

The man's canoe had been tied to the bank, but because of the heavy tropical rains, the river had risen a number of feet and his canoe had been swept away by the current. The missionary asked if I wanted to go with him in his outboard powered canoe. How excited I was to have my first trip into the jungle. It was a little difficult hiding my excitement. So off we went; one missionary, one young rookie and five primitive tribesmen.

Rick & Jeff's Professional Landscape Company

6
Into the Jungle

From the village it was only a ten minute walk to the river. We walked down the trail to where we got into the small dugout canoe and started down the river.

I sat carefully between the Indians, the missionary in the rear operating the motor. As we continued down the narrow, swiftly moving river, I attempted to take in my new surroundings.

A recent high school graduate, I soon realized that school had taught me little to prepare me for these uncivilized surroundings. The jungle, from all I could see, was a tangled mass of trees and vines, palms and thorns. The dark green curtain reached to the river's edge and at times appeared to be a long, dark alley. For the most part I could only imagine all that lurked beyond the surface. And imagine I did!

I had been told about the jungle. For a novice, it was a bit difficult imagining just how many alligators, jaguars, poisonous snakes, boa constrictors, stinging ants, big spiders, scorpions and other attacking creatures might be waiting behind the first layer of foliage.

The further we traveled, the more irrelevant my calculations became as I began to wonder how far we were leaving the village behind. I figured that walking by trail we were perhaps days away! What will we do if the canoe sinks? How will we get back? What if the Indians get hungry and we are the only meat around? How would I ever know if they wanted to eat us, since I couldn't understand their language? What difference would it make anyhow, since there is nowhere to run? I continued to think through my many questions as I watched the water rush by. Hey, I wonder if there are piranhas in the water.

It was late afternoon and the sun was quickly dropping behind the mountain. There was still a lot of light, but it would be getting dark very soon. The jungle was already a mass of shadows. I was still working on acting calm and collected. I took a quick glance back at the missionary to see the look on his face. Most of us have the subconscious habit of looking to the one who is a leader when we feel nervous or unsure. On my part it was definitely not a habit, nor was it subconscious. I was nervous and knew it. So I looked back at the missionary who had that typical missionary look, the kind card players have whenever holding a winning hand or trying to bluff one into thinking they do!

Disappointed, I returned my look again toward the front of the dugout. Shortly thereafter, we came to a sharp turn in the river where the Indians spotted the lost canoe. It had been caught by the current and thrown into some tree branches protruding from the dark water. This would be my first very basic lesson on the jungle.

In many places throughout the Amazon region and, more specifically, on smaller tributaries fed by rushing mountain streams, the waters quickly rise and fall. As tropical rainstorms hit the mountains up river, torrents of water rush down, filling smaller streams and tributaries. In many areas, as these tributaries fill, they overflow the banks, covering great expanses of jungle floor.

This creates an interesting phenomena of nature. It doesn't take a scientist to figure out what might happen to the millions of small creatures, insects, spiders, etc. that normally live and crawl on the jungle floor. They either have to run, slither, hop, scamper, drown or venture up the closest branch, vine or tree for protection from the rising waters. Because many smaller creatures aren't equipped for long marathon escapes and many are not very fast at hopping, slithering and the like, a quick escape in most cases is not likely. Also, since most of these creatures are fairly efficient in their constant fight for survival, most do not go down without a battle. For the majority, then, the easiest solution is simply ascending the nearest jungle growth to avoid the temporary flood waters. This results in an area where most of the crawling creatures that are normally scattered and dispersed over a vast jungle floor are now competing for a parking spot on the foliage and lower jungle branches that are slowly being covered by the rising flood waters.

Another interesting aspect of the constantly changing jungle is its soil consistency. Contrary to common thought, most parts of the Amazon do not have a deep fertile layer of top soil. To one living in the Amazon, it is not uncommon to hear large trees fall from time to time, pulling up their massive but shallow root structures. As the rivers rise and fall, trees also are swept away by fast-moving currents.

It would have been fortunate had I understood these and other characteristics of the mysterious jungle region. Certainly it would have made those first few hours in the jungle a bit more enjoyable. Then again, if I had known too much more, I might have been a bit more nervous. Years later, a young friend was killed by a jaguar further down river, and another Indian I knew was snatched out of his canoe by an anaconda while fishing.

We struggled in keeping our canoe upright in the swift current, while attempting to reach the Indian's dugout with a tow line. With the rope attached, the missionary started the outboard and pointed our canoe headfirst into the current. Because of the flood waters, we were actually over the bank.

The outboard motor became tangled in vines and branches under the water's surface and stalled. The swift current turned us broadside and carried us into a tree which was leaning towards the river. The strength of the river running under us broadside rolled our small canoe, tipping it into the oncoming waters. Ultimately, we got our canoe straightened out. I looked back to the missionary hoping to see some expression of confidence. No such luck! We tried again with the same frightening results. The Indians continued to gibber back and forth, but, of course, I had absolutely no idea what was being said! Looking back again, I saw no change in the missionary's poker face!

Before I knew it, we were taking a new course of action, for me no more preferred than the first. I was no longer trying to impress the missionary with a valiant composure. My efforts were now more focused on just staying in the dugout. We had untied the Indian's canoe and had begun pulling ourselves away from the river into the dark and tangled vine-filled swamp. I had no idea what we were doing or where we were heading. I joined the Indians grabbing vines, trees and branches as we pulled ourselves deeper into this dark humid swamp.

My efforts to maintain a mature and calm composure were quickly diminishing. I left the pulling and pushing to the Indians and dedicated myself to killing, brushing off and avoiding as many spiders and other multi-legged creatures as possible. I was quick to notice that the Indians also were bummed by the biting invaders. They were swatting and smashing as many as possible. Meanwhile, they continued pulling us deeper into the swamp.

I had the feeling that we were not only out-numbered by the creatures boarding our canoe, we were also their meal, a smorgasbord of both white and dark meat. There were at first little spiders, then larger ones, with some large enough to cover one's face with body and legs. My efforts were more dedicated to the latter. We were all being bitten. I took another look back at the missionary; no words, just that poker face and some newly added smashed bugs and spiders to his forehead.

A short time later we broke out of the swamp and I finally understood the reasoning of our Indian friends for entering it. The river had risen so high that much of the water had been flowing over a peninsula of land which created a turn in the river. Now instead of being on the outside, most swift part of the river, we were on the inside calmer waters.

It took a little while to finish killing the rest of the uninvited hitchhikers, but we were finally left in peace. Now we could see a beautiful stretch of river with the rapids not far beyond. We could hear the water rushing over the rocks below. I was relieved to be out of the swamp and on our way back to the village. After clearing the vines and branches out of the outboard motor prop and securing our Indian boat in tow, we were off. The missionary started his outboard motor and we were on our way.

Oh, how glad I was to be heading back! As we came around the first bend, the current was quite swift because of the proximity to the rapids. We were moving ever so slowly when the motor started to cough and miss. This time, looking back at the missionary, I saw the same poker face but now more on the pale side. As the motor began missing, our headway slowed to a halt. We were neither advancing nor were we sliding back towards the rapids.

Be not deceived of any great bravery on my part. I was thinking very much of the rapids and thought it an appropriate time for a prayer meeting. Since the Indians were simply holding on, looking straight ahead, and the missionary had enough to do driving the motor, I ventured to begin the one-man prayer meeting on my own. Before I started to pray, the chattering of the Indians brought my attention to a giant uprooted tree which was turning and twisting in the turbulent currents of the river ahead. Before I could begin my little prayer meeting, I noted that this giant tree would soon smash right into our dwarfed dugout and carry us down the rapids. There was now no time to pray; just hold on to the edges of the canoe. Here it comes!

As the current twisted the giant tree, it made a big turn, missing our canoe and smashing into the canoe in tow. I was quite frazzled, to say the least. Even the Indians looked pale and were obviously upset. It was time to quickly pray that we would avoid joining the tree as it plummeted toward the rapids and falls.

It was an intense prayer meeting, probably a bit more begging and pleading than real peaceful prayer. There was not time to "be still and know I am God." It was much more a last ditch effort to remind God that we were in a bit of need.

My prayer was answered. We began to move, the first turn directing us toward the place where we originally recovered the lost dugout. As we approached, the Indians began to point and comment about our experience there. The pointing and comments were suddenly interrupted by a loud cracking sound that overcame the roar of the rapids and sounds of the struggling outboard. A huge tree crashed across the river as the current eroded its foundation. It was totally discouraging to see it completely flatten everything in its path, including the branches and trees we were holding for security just minutes before. I looked back to see the countenance of the missionary, still poker faced.

I prayed all the way back to the trail and was glad to again arrive at the base. I was asked to carry the gas tank out of the canoe and up the bank. It felt a bit light; I opened it and found no gas. We had returned on a tank of prayer!

That night was a sobering one for me. Late into the night, I stared out into the jungle and into the sky which from time to time lit up from distant lightning. A multitude of noises filled the jungle. An environment tamed by knowledge and understanding, yet to an outsider, a mysterious world.

7

Perspectives Challenged

The next day, Jeff and the new missionary arrived with the final supplies. We began right away constructing this missionary's house. Both Jeff and I were in for some survival lessons which often led to our being more stupid than brave.

For awhile, we camped some distance from the base, down through the valley, up a portion of the river and then upstream toward a large waterfall. This led to a trail that took us to a cedar tree we were milling with a chain saw mill.

One day, we took off into the jungle chasing a wild turkey. As I bumped into a tree, a one-inch long stinging ant fell onto my back, sinking its powerful stinger into my flesh. This quickly dampened enthusiasm for our hunting trip.

After hunting down and shooting the turkey, we returned to our small jungle camp which was nothing more than some large leaves laid over a simple frame of tree limbs, covering our hammocks. Jeff and I were all alone. The new missionary was making some difficult adaptations himself and had returned to the base to bury his pet dog which had not done well with jungle living.

It had been raining all day; everything was wet. We gathered what wood we could to cook the turkey. After hanging the turkey from the roof of our little shelter, we managed to start a small fire, but after a smoky start, it refused to continue burning. After numerous failed attempts, we decided a little gasoline would help. Charred on the outside, still bloody on the inside, the turkey fell from the roof into the blazing fire which leaped to the height of the roof. As the gasoline fire burned down, there was our turkey, covered with mud and soot. Jeff and I stared at our dinner turkey, a bit of steam ascending from an entrée prepared by master chefs. The burned vine that was supposed to hold our turkey hung limply from the roof poles. We reorganized our kitchen area and, with a little more chain saw gas, we completed the cooking.

One day after we had moved back to the base, an Indian came to the missionary's house talking up a storm about something. The missionary understood enough to realize that a child in a village over the mountain had been bitten by a snake. He figured the village to be only a few hours hike away. The two missionaries and Jeff put together a small medical kit and took off. I was sick with malaria, and, although I wanted to go, I was too weak. The short trip turned into a three-day ordeal in which the men had to climb up steep jungle slopes, sliding down the other side. Arriving at a small jungle dwelling, they found the child badly in need of medical attention. They did what they could and ended up saving the child's life.

The trip back was so bad that at one point it was doubtful that one of the missionaries would make it. As they slowly made their way back, some tribal men emerged on the trail. They offered the guys some corn drink they had. It had fermented and smelled rancid. Jeff was extremely thirsty and quickly accepted the drink. He drank it down, only to throw it all up a short time after.

For three days I battled continually with increasing fevers and was on my back on the floor sick when the door creaked open. There stood Jeff, covered with mud. He stepped in and fell to the floor. When the missionary came in, he didn't look any better and couldn't even speak. To save the child's life, Jeff and the missionaries risked losing their own.

The jungle people, their fears, their all-night chanting, their daily lives interested us greatly. Apart from all of our nonsense, joking and lighthearted spirits, we were also greatly burdened. Pages cannot hold the lessons God was impressing on our hearts.

The word "lost" took on a meaning we had not known before. The meaning of pain became more real than we had understood before. The level of dedication and commitment of the missionary servants we observed there in the jungle was something we had rarely seen in the land from which we had come. These families had few of those things which most in our country consider as basic necessities. They were not the happy-go-lucky seminary graduates we had first envisioned, skipping around with pith-helmets and butterfly nets, but rather, serious individuals laboring to bring an option and answer of eternal life to a small group of Indians, otherwise spiritually lost in the middle of the jungle. Forever lost.

Before leaving the jungle, we would see many

other needs and villages which wanted missionaries. A world of great need, a world needing so much the message of salvation and the action of the church. A world so close, though, separated by many miles of religious nonsense, fancy church programs, senseless church building expansions, ingrown fellowships and home-grown "needs" including organ committees, bell choir tours and the like.

There were many nights and days, working in the jungle, when Jeff and I spoke with one another of issues of far-reaching spiritual consequences. We prayed together daily as we listened to God. God was forming our lives in ways we would not understand as young men.

For Jeff, this would lead him to a life of committed service in numerous arenas including pastoring a church in California, heading up a very successful manufacturing company with a partner in North Carolina and working with various foreign mission efforts in South America and Mexico including our own. It's unfortunate that in our country we draw a distinct line between "Christian work" and "secular work." Over the last decades I have seen Jeff's work in both, and he as well as his work has been the same--one of sacrifice, service, help and concern for others. Jeff's unquestioned integrity and upright character have inspired many, including me.

For me, these formative times would lead to a slightly different path. God was working us through a process. This was a process of struggle and testing which the apostle Paul spoke of with great confidence to the Philippians. "For I am confident of this very thing, that He who began a *good work* in you will perfect it until the day of Christ Jesus." It was this "good work," as Paul calls it, that I would soon come to hate and challenge.

Before Jeff and I completed our trip, we passed through some other areas of the Amazon territory where we experienced other challenges and learned from different missionaries and Indians. Little did we know that the demand for flexibility and adaptation to the jungle would be much easier than reversing the process, returning to our own country. It wasn't that our homeland had changed that much in the short time we were gone as much as our own world view and perspective that had changed.

We both returned sick. Jeff came back 30 pounds lighter with a strand of twine holding his pants up. It's fascinating how, as we all go through life, our view of things can change so drastically. The Wednesday before departing for South America, a Christian rock band entertained the youth group with popular music. The night we returned, we went straight from the airport to church; the same band, the same music, the same screaming crowd. This time it seemed like something was wrong. Not just this but other things that seemed normal and wholesome before the trip, now seemed very empty and without purpose. Many of the activities which previously seemed like great ideas now seemed to almost mock the idea that these would be called outreaches or ministries. We were seeing things differently than before, and whether or not we liked it, it was just the way it was.

The problem of confronting these questions was very much our own, since it was we who had a change of perspective. We were, no doubt, over-zealous, idealistic and simplistic in our views. There seemed to be something inherently wrong with the idea that church decoration committees and stained glass had much to do with the Bible or that God's Word had much to do with these things.

Perhaps some of these activities distracted our attention from reaching out to the suffering and needy. Is not the purpose of "church" the equipping of the saints for the work of service, to the building up of the body of Christ, through each one using and learning to use his or her gifts (Ephesians 4:11-12)? Only then can there be fertile ground upon which we can talk, in any serious sense, about outreach to lost neighbors, needy people on the street, the sick or crippled, or the lost tribes in the jungle.

"*Go therefore and make disciples of all nations,.....
I am with you always, even to the end of the age.*"
Matthew 28:19-20

The questions lingered. What were these voids between what we saw to be Biblical truth and our actual pursuits in life? This had bothered me before, but now I was more certain than ever that my own life was quite out of line.

I wanted to see my life lived out according to truth, but all the time being painfully aware of my shortcomings. At the same time I held the idea that our North American churches somehow had more life-changing outreach and ministry potential than that normally utilized.

Jeff meets Yanomamö, 1979

Rick with Yanomamö, 1979

Jeff at break during war, 1980

8
Discrepancies

On our return, Jeff and I were invited to speak in various churches, youth meetings, camps and conferences about what we had seen, learned and experienced in the South American jungle. Reality hit, however, and we realized that little of what we felt or learned could be spiritually conveyed or appreciated. As blind as we were at the young age of 18, we somehow believed that Christians everywhere would be enthusiastic and excited to find that there are real and urgent needs that they could effectively fill and meet almost immediately. We soon realized that in most cases there was much more interest in the artifacts we brought back than in the primitive tribesmen who had fashioned them.

So who cared about these tribesmen who might respond with profound joy to the great message of God's Word if someone would only go to tell them? Jeff and I were both consumed with a feeling of great urgency to make known the needs waiting beneath the thick jungle canopy. We were also consumed with an ever increasing sense of loneliness as we found that interest in reaching these lost tribes was slight.

At one conference in a western state, we finished speaking and opened the platform to questions. We began to laugh as one woman voiced her question, but soon our laugher became dignified throat clearing. We quickly noted that her question was a serious one and not meant to be a joke. "Why spend all the time and work to teach these people? Couldn't a blimp be deployed to these tribes, equipped with a large flannel graph? Missionaries could communicate God's Word in a matter of minutes using a giant flannel graph covered blimp hovering above the villages."

We took a couple deep breaths before trying to answer her question. The quickest answer would have simply been that the Indians would shoot the blimp out of the sky with their seven foot arrows, but that would no doubt stimulate further questions of this type. The need for basic mission education in that church seemed monumental.

We began hosting an increasing number of groups into our own ministry field in Mexico for a more in-depth look and orientation concerning world missions. It was our strong conviction to challenge others to join in some way in the task of world missions. It was fulfilling to see different people respond, a good number of whom are now serving as missionaries overseas or in other ministries.

One of the greatest spiritual conflicts we observed during those first years was how quickly the vision of many youth and adults was drowned in a swamp of busy activities once they returned home. I was reminded of my earlier years; so little of church had anything to do with any relationship with Jesus Christ. The important things were those surrounding the local church: being a good church attendee, giving to expand the church facilities, contributing to buy a new organ or piano, entertainment programs, etc. No wonder the world can't relate to some churches; some churches aren't very relevant to the world. Is it any wonder para-church organizations flourish?

Most churches with which we were in contact were more interested in missions awareness than missions involvement, exposing the church to a quick glimpse of world need rather than opening the collective church to meeting those needs, being informed of facts and figures concerning world missions rather than actually being actively concerned with doing anything constructive. Certainly much of our evangelical world has created an unfavorable environment for healthy Christianity to flourish.

Few of our organized church activities have much to do with New Testament living. Commitment, dedication, purpose, sacrificial work and serious giving are words that characterized, in a unique way, a lifestyle we had witnessed within some of those with whom we had lived. This had seriously challenged Jeff and me, yet in being asked to share these things with different groups, we were left feeling that this provided only good discussion material for camps or retreats. Those daring to apply too much commitment, dedication or sacrifice to their personal lives would be reminded that this was discussion material only, not to be out of balance.

This great separation between our spiritual or "church life" and our secular or outside life is a mystery seemingly propagated by many preachers. It seems amazing that many Christians believe to varying degrees that "normal" Christians live under one set of expectations and standards, while missionaries and pastors live under another. In a number of ways this may be true, yet the basis of the idea might be suspect. While missionaries need a special calling from God to do what they are doing, "regular people" apparently need no calling to do whatever pleases them in life, as long as they attend church and put money in the offering plate.

Since this calling could never actually be described as such, the obvious course of action would be to encourage and teach youth and adult groups to live good lives, be faithful church goers, pray God's blessings upon every plan and desire and be generous as God prospers them. It sounds so Godly, but what a sham! Instead of seeking first the Kingdom of God, we seek first our kingdom and how God might fit into it. Popular preaching teaches us how God might neatly fit into our lives rather than how we might conform our lives to His.

Many tangles of traditional evangelical teaching and accommodations have made the revolutionary teachings and life of Jesus Christ quite clouded. This problem in many North American evangelical circles would soon become a personal battle. To put things in perspective, I knew that I was no more spiritual than anyone else and that if anyone needed a change of heart, it was I.

I had always assumed that I was a disciple of Christ, but what was the bottom line that dictated my life and decisions? Paul said, *"I have been crucified with Christ. And it is no longer I who live but Christ lives in me"* (Galatians 2:20).

As well as I thought I understood what Paul was saying, it was far from reality in my actual living. However, as I write this page while traveling with an Indian friend on another long river trip to a village in these Amazon headwaters, it is far from me. In the midst of "missionary living," serving Christ, going on difficult trips "for the Lord," doing what some consider sacrificial service, I need to be very clear. Concerning being crucified with Christ (Galatians 2.20), I can attain this, on a daily basis, only when I have my life submitted to His. Because of my sinful nature, which I cannot excuse, I can honestly say today that I relate better to what Paul says in Philippians 3:13-14, *"I do not regard myself as having laid hold of it yet; but one thing I do: forgetting what lies behind and reaching forward to what lies ahead, I press on toward the goal for the prize of the upward call of God in Christ Jesus."*

Certainly I have no excuse. It is by God's mercy that I am even alive today. By His life and mercy, I have been given life to live for Him, although many times I've made a sad show of it.

Rick at age 18 working in Amazon

Rick and Jeff returning from South America, 1979

9
Sickness, Brokenness and Depression

When Jeff and I returned from South America, I was more than just a bit sick, a condition which seemed normal considering our life in the jungle. I went to a community college to register for classes the day after returning.

I never expected culture shock upon coming back to my own homeland. So many people, confusion, lines, registration numbers, and I was sick. I didn't last 30 minutes before giving up; I simply couldn't function. It was as if I were placed in a foreign land of which I understood nothing. I drove home defeated. A friend returned with me to help me register. All I remember was telling him to sign me up for any classes at all, and I signed the papers.

Within the first week after our return, I saw the doctor. My visits to the doctor were frequent. During those first visits, he checked out the basic, expected problems: parasites, worms, infections, malaria. Seemingly easy enough. Not one week would pass in the next seven months that I would not be plagued by sickness.

Spots which appeared like a rash of bleeding beneath the skin migrated over my body. At times it felt as if swarms of ants were released in my head. Skin ulcers and boils, internal bleeding, fevers and chills, infections and a mysterious neck and throat swelling plagued me.

I was attending college classes in the mornings but working afternoons in construction and home remodeling. There were times when I became too sick and dizzy to work. Sitting to rest a few minutes, I often fell asleep, waking up just minutes later shaking and sweating, other times clammy and cold. I tried to take it all in stride, but God had a process through which to take me.

For all of us, I am convinced God wants to test the quality of our faith and at the same time build for Himself servants of pure heart. What a painful process it can be. As in military boot camp for the soldier, God has a time or times to test and mature us, through hardship, pain, sorrow, sufferings, trials, persecution, to bring us toward perfection. Take a look at James 1:2-4.

"Consider it all joy my brethren when you encounter various trials, knowing that the testing of your faith produces endurance, and let endurance have its perfect result, that you may be perfect and complete lacking in nothing."

The "counting it all joy" part has always been hard for me. These times of testing or maturing can be painfully long. Praise the Lord for the many examples He has given us in His Word of many who victoriously found God to be sufficient in their lives: Moses, Abraham, Job; Hebrews chapter 11 lists many others. But still, many times in the midst of our personal testings, we find little comfort in knowing others have walked similar paths, even more so when we need to be broken of our pride, self-sufficiency and self-esteem.

And so, far removed from my understanding, God needed to teach me something, and it would take a number of months to begin to learn some of those lessons.

At first, my infirmities were easier to accept. After about six weeks, however, I became disturbed; it didn't seem right that God would allow this after I had faithfully served him. Every week though a different or repeating sickness; going to the doctor became an embarrassment.

I was eighteen years old entering a dark season of life which would forever change me. I understand now, however, that if this time had been any less difficult, it would have been of no positive effect in my life. At the time however, the many visits to the doctor, a tropical disease hospital, more examinations, more medications, all led to failures and discouragements.

My impatience with God turned to bitterness. Frankly I became sick of people praising the Lord; the singing in church services made my stomach turn. Sarcasm at its best!

"What a nice day," someone commented. I was quick to give that individual another point of view!

Few braved speaking to me after observing my bitterness. There were a few faithful friends who stuck by me even though I don't know why they felt compelled to do so. Certainly these days helped to form the perspective I hold today of true friendship.

I became not only discouraged and depressed but disappointed with God. There were those who came as spiritual lifeguards, throwing spiritual lifesavers, all of which sank below me. Others were sincere and caring but perhaps a step ahead of God's timing.

Most of us have known the feeling of desperation. I was desperate. The ongoing sicknesses, physical fatigue, discouragement and alienation I experienced were profoundly affecting my spirit. I was slowly losing my desire for this "Christian living." I was jealous of others who appeared to have God working in their lives. I never doubted God's existence--that I could see--but God's face was set against me and He wouldn't tell me why. God was unfair; that I could prove with little effort. Although God had become to me the Great One with power to oppress me for something He would not give me the chance to reconcile, I still believed that somehow, some way, a victorious life could be obtained. I grabbed onto any advice that was offered.

Suffering knocks on the door of each of our lives. It comes in different measures and wears many masks. For me, any physical suffering seemed of little importance in contrast to the depth of disappointment which was growing as I realized that God was not the Loving One I had perceived Him to be. I felt all but drowned in my faith and my Christian experience.

If you should ever cross a similar desert, may you be spared the many well-intentioned counselors.

And so it went--lots of lifesavers, lots of well-intentioned counselors. For my physical challenges I continued to seek medical help. For where the rivers of my physical, mental and spiritual sufferings ran together, I gave my efforts to grabbing onto whatever counsel I was given.

"Rick, you are trying to deal with all these things in your own strength. You need to put all these things in God's hands and rest in Him. Don't be so intense. Have faith and wait upon the Lord. Quit trying to make things happen with God; let Him do it," I was told.

That sounded right, I thought. Was this the answer? Rest in the Lord. Of course, He is trying to teach me something. That's it! Slack off, trust and go with the flow. Trust and obey, there's no other way....

Even as I put these things in God's hands like fragile, fine china, I could hear them all hit the floor with a crash. My bitterness increased.

I returned to my regular routine of trying to pray and figure things out from the Bible, but I was getting no better response than if praying to a dead tree. As for reading, well, God wasn't giving me any beautiful new insights, to say the least. On the contrary, every page held discouragement and empty promises. But there was help, just in time, as my head was raised by another helping hand.

"Brother, this is no way to handle this conflict.

Yes, you need to trust, but you can't just go with the flow and see what happens. This is a serious matter, one that needs to be approached in searching prayer, fasting and seeking in the Word."

That's it! A bigger sacrifice on my part, I thought. By really giving it my best effort, somehow I would find the link causing the sickness, the bitterness and the great emptiness in my soul.

I fasted, prayed and searched with all sincerity and honesty. There were results; however, they were a bit less than expected. The fasting made me hungry, the reading made me feel mocked and my prayers echoed through dark empty halls.

God did not respond to my prayers; praying was an exercise in futility and frustration. Reading the Word was worse. There was Jesus, the Healer, but I was not healed. There was Jesus the compassionate One, yet I felt no compassion as I sought Him in hurt, sickness, depression and pain. There was Jesus doing good and responding to need but I was in need calling to Him and to no avail. The fasting only built a wall of isolation and frustration around me.

"Rick, have you read Job? He is a man who went through incredible trials. Read chapters 1-2 and 42!"

Job is a great Old Testament book and these selected chapters were just what I needed. In the first two chapters Job is stripped of everything he owns. In chapter 42 God blesses Job two-fold.

But as you can imagine, at this point I was far from believing that God was going to bring any blessing upon me. The more I sought after the Lord, the further away He seemed to be. There is a lot of history between chapters 2 and 42! Job wasn't the man we have heard about in a lot of modern day "follow God to riches" teaching! I found an emotional Job, which at the time was of no encouragement to me. In chapter 3, verse 1, Job cursed the day of his birth and that was just the beginning! I empathized with Job who felt God was unjust.

I said earlier that there were a few faithful friends. Their advice was not so flashy but eternally more sound.

"I don't understand. All I can say is stay faithful and hang in there," they would say.

Twice over seven months an infection took over my neck and throat. The doctor couldn't diagnose the problem and called his associate for consultation. My neck was swollen from my chin to my chest, choking my breathing and swallowing. If this was God's idea of blessing His children, I had had enough. I was taking heavy doses of antibiotics with no results. Many were praying for me; however, I saw this was obviously only a useless ritual.

The second time this problem arose I didn't go back to the doctor right away. There was a man coming to town, well respected and well-known, who spoke all over the country on Satan and demonic forces. He came to San Diego and I went to hear him speak. Perhaps he had some insights. I planned on speaking to him afterwards, but I didn't have to approach him. When he was finished speaking, he came looking for me!

Rick and Jeff working to build missionary house, 1980

10

Faith or Fiction

The speaker had heard about me and the oppression upon me. He asked a lot of questions and we spoke for quite some time. It was fairly late when we finished our conversation. He looked me in the eye and said God wanted to deliver me from this oppression and to heal me that very night.

My soul was desperate. I so deeply desired for this to be true. He told me I must believe and, you know, I really tried. We prayed together and a wonderful sense of peace and assurance came over me. He placed his hands on me and prayed for deliverance and healing. In all my hope I could almost feel the change. I was grateful; I thanked him and hurried out to the parking lot. Instead of driving home, I went to the bay. As I pulled up to the edge of the bay, I watched the city lights reflecting on the water. Out of hope and faith I began to praise God for my healing. This went on for awhile before I reached up to feel my healed neck. When I reached to touch it I found that I had only built up my hope or faith for nothing. I was definitely not healed and by no means was I delivered from the oppression. On the contrary, I was even more bitter, deceived, frustrated and depressed. My faith had let me down. The well-known expert was no doubt sincere and loving; however, he was sincerely deceived in thinking that I would be freed from any afflictions that night.

Looking back now, I think a lot of the hope I

latched onto were wonderful, good things I had grown up hearing. Good things that, because of their good nature, somehow got grafted into Christian teaching. Apparently few ask if, just because an idea is good, is it necessarily true?

In reflecting now, I must say that I believe that much of our modern day Christian faith is not so Christian at all. Many of us live in or pass through times of crushing disappointment, discouragement or despair during our lives. Has God abandoned us? In our process of learning, one thing can be said for sure; our pains do not necessarily lead us closer to virtue, yet they inevitably lead us closer to truth. This, I believe, is an important principle from which James speaks in the first chapter of his epistle.

Could it be that much of our frustration comes from the bitter realization that much of our faith is just that, our faith, not at all God's? Our hopes and expectations drawn from childhood fairy tales are mixed with enough of God's Word to give us a fair balance of eternal heaven and a bit of heaven on earth.

Now, after twenty-five years working within the ranks of the poor and the primitive, I see more clearly that it is those of western society who seem to struggle more acutely with these issues of why there is so much suffering in the world, or why bad things happen to those we perceive as so undeserving of misfortune. It is in this statement that we discover a confused "Christian precept" built up in our so-called "Christian sub-culture"--

that which portrays bad people as deserving of misfortune and good people as worthy of good fortune.

No doubt this was a subconscious idea of my own at the time I was so sick and struggling. My intentions were good, I wanted to be a good person, a good Christian, to serve others and do everything possible to help   others, I couldn't understand   why   my   life   was   so cursed. The problem stares us in the eye. Why do we see ourselves as so wonderful and deserving? As soon as we ask, "Why me?" or "Why my good friend?" we are already asking the wrong question.

In brief, it has nothing to do with merit. If it did, we would all have been eliminated by now! It seems that in many ways, God's Word has less influence on the Christian community than does our altered and more attractive version of it. Yes, our version is more attractive! Look in Christian bookstores.

Shelves of books and materials, many leading you after   a   mirage   of   more   blessings,   material satisfaction, positive thinking, good health and good fortune--all Christian, of course.

Perhaps I stand against the current here, but it certainly appears that many popular Christian publications   and   materials   are   much   more egocentric than God-centric; a lot of "good" stuff for sale. How much of it is really true? It probably doesn't matter as long as it is "Christian" and people are buying it.

During those months which stretched into years of sickness, I now recognize that I was a believer but had never really wrestled through a lot of what I believed. You may relate to this. That which we believe, is best demonstrated in how we use our discretionary time and money. Challenges, hardships and persecution can force us to some healthy re-evaluation of our life values and beliefs. My struggles and sicknesses threw me into a prolonged process of evaluation and searching. Part of this process awakened a sense of hypocrisy in my thinking. For years I had believed different things simply because it was convenient to do so. We all do this. There is a danger in how this can infect our connectedness to reality, leading to a great disparity between what we say we believe and how we actually live. This was a complicated struggle for an 18 year old.

The following example seems extreme but may be all too common. I picked up a Christian magazine recently which held an example of how we can be swayed by disparity, inconsistent faith and emotions. I quote the advertisement, "...Christian Cruise Vacations, 7 glorious days and nights" etc. etc. A big photo, in color, of a beautiful cruise ship, swimming pools and all the food one could eat. From $995, all inclusive! On the next page, a black and white photo of a poor suffering woman. I quote "...for only $10 a month your love will provide weekly food, medicine, blankets, a bed, and small monthly allowance." Hard to believe that a poor widowed woman can get all that glorious help for $10 a month while a normal

Christian will pay $1000 for only seven glorious days and nights! All inclusive, of course! That includes cruising with nationally known Christian speakers and dynamic Christian recording artists. These extras are not included for the starving woman.

Now, in no way am I trying to communicate that it is wrong to go on a cruise. That's fine! Let's all go and have a great time. I'm more inclined to believe we can have a great cruise for $1000 than I am to believe that any mission organization can buy all those supplies for the poor starving widow for "only $10 a month!" What I am saying is we simply need to be honestly real and at the same time, really honest. We would do well to make sure that what we seek, how we live, how we administer our funds, how we spend our days and how we perceive life fits what is appropriate and acceptable for us as followers of Christ.

During this particular time, understanding the Christian life was a great problem for me. I could not define it at the time, but my idea of what God's part was and what my part was just didn't fit. God was letting me down. The Christian life was not working as I expected it to. Over the past more than 25 years, I have spoken with countless others who also found that their model of faith failed them terribly in their moment of need. Although I believe that this model is the result of a process and is under constant change as we spiritually mature, I find a great paradox.

Jesus praised those of simple faith, the children,

those who had few questions as they stepped out with unshaken confidence. Nevertheless, each of us strives for a deeper understanding of our faith. We spend a lifetime searching through the depths for the answers to so many complex questions. Those who seem to have become most mature are those who appear to have come full circle. Whether they set out studying philosophy, history, theology, sociology, anthropology or other disciplines including endless Christian study, they inevitably return. They return to the trust of a child, the silence of one ignorant in the face of the vast greatness of the Great Almighty Creator. This in turn brings one to humbly kneel before God. I am in an active pursuit of this "degeneration" as I will call it.

Pre-raid dance

11

Back to the Amazon?

Some things are not easily explained. A year had passed, and Jeff and I were on our way back to South America. A missionary from our church was to begin work in a village in the jungle lowlands. "Why go back?" was not a question I asked. I was compelled from within, although it might sound unreasonable.

Although everything in my personal life seemed to be cursed, God apparently was blessing the preparation to make our journey back to the Amazon. There were many doubts, fears and bitter feelings which I held quietly inside as best I could. We organized various activities and raised funds to buy a large chain saw and mill to cut lumber in the jungle. I continued to be sick. Poor Mom and Dad! They put up with a lot. Jeff had to always give the "right" answer for us when we were asked spiritual questions; I was too cynical.

As the departure date neared I had great doubts that I would live much longer. I made a simple will and letter for family and my few friends. It was extremely difficult saying good-bye to everyone at the airport. I believed I would not see them again. I was sure that the resolution to my sunken being would soon be brought to completion one way or another.

I felt angry at God, yet very much at His mercy.

Jeff and I checked all the equipment and baggage on the airline, got through security, said all our good-byes and settled down in our plane seats.

It was quiet. Jeff is a good friend; he knew that I was not going to be of any spiritual encouragement to him. When it came to me and spiritual matters Jeff would be quiet for the most part; he quietly and constantly prayed for me.

Although there was great provision for all of our needed work equipment, Jeff and I were on a limited personal budget. That meant we would have to improvise. That could mean anything to two 18 year old youths still wanting to test and try everything. Our long layover in Miami was too long.

After pestering the Hare Krishna who were selling their books at the airport, we became bored and decided to get a few hours sleep. The only quiet place we could find was on one of the luggage carousels. We slept well until the police shined their lights in on us and pulled us out for a complete police check. I laughed at Jeff while he was being questioned. That was all he needed as he tried to keep a straight face. Finally, we both straightened up with a serious Rick and Jeff Landscape professional posture and emotionally apologized for falling asleep on the carousel and overlooking the great danger of being swept away with the luggage on the conveyor belt.

When any adversity would face us, somehow we would find a way to make the best of it. Such was the case when we finally arrived at the Caracas international airport only to find that our luggage had been accidentally put on a plane to Brazil. At first we were devastated, but it didn't take long for us to figure out that this might mean that the airline may owe us a fancy hotel room until they came up with our luggage. I'm sure our young age lent to the fact that much of life could be adjusted to our liking. Being young,   you don't have to accept some problems; you just improvise. If anything goes wrong, you have an excuse—you are too young to know better!

There was a bit of a line at the complaint desk. Those that had the most difficult time getting to the desk were the non-Venezuelans. But Jeff and I already knew the procedure. We learned from our first trip, if you want help or service, you need to show it. So, one of us would stand as close to the counter as possible and the other push. We were soon in fair competing position. When we finally reached the counter, I guess we lacked the business-like, dignified appearance that would have helped. We were the only kids at the desk; we didn't have a suit or tie but we still did as the others, banging our fist on the desk demanding a hotel. No way was the airline going to put up two kids. They thought it would be too easy to bump us.

They told us to go on and they would forward our bags to us later. We had worked in Latin America enough to know how that goes. We would never again see our bags, so we would wait right there. It was after midnight when we set up camp in front of the airline's office door. The gentleman who had attended us at the complaint desk finally came back. He yelled at us for sitting on the floor in front of the office door and did not take us seriously. We just put on sad faces and told him how hungry we were. He went in the office and shut the door. We sat right in front of the door. Soon both the day and night shift knew us well, as we greeted each worker going and coming through the door.

When the night shift came back, our friend arrived again and was a bit surprised to find us still there. Rene was his name. Late that next night, Rene lightened up and asked us if we would like to come into the office. He must have felt sorry for us, but that was his mistake! He asked us if we knew how to use their fancy airline coffee maker.

"Of course," we chirped back, "we do this all the time."

Shooting practice—essential for survival

12

Luggage Cart Ride to a Caribbean Vacation!

While Rene was busy at work, Jeff and I were trying to figure out why water and coffee were boiling over the counter. All the phones were ringing, so while I completed the disaster with the coffee maker, Jeff started answering the phones. He did real well considering he couldn't communicate with the Spanish speaking callers! He was, however, just charming in English. Rene was pulling his hair out, but I think we were a breath of fresh air for him at the same time.

Rene again encouraged us to continue our travel without our bags. He promised that they were on their way. We still had our doubts, so, we assured him that we would be living in front of the office door until they arrived. Rene stepped out for a moment. When he returned, I think he was even more convinced of the need to get rid of us. By this time, Jeff and I were on the airline computers pushing all the buttons.

"What are you guys doing?" he yelled. Casually glancing up from the screen, we informed Rene that we were looking for our suitcases. Rene was getting tired so, we thought we would show Rene how to give real scary rides on the luggage carts. I think the luggage cart incident was too much for him.

With that and a few other stunts, Rene had had enough! He left for a few minutes to obtain the needed signatures and then returned. He took

Jeff and me to a phone where there was a tourist directory of hotels and resorts. We had already heard about one resort where there was five-star service, water sports, room service, two swimming pools, rooms on the beach and more.

So when Rene told us to find a hotel, we didn't need to pray about which one. We made the call with visions in mind of bikini clad girls popping grapes in our mouths, breakfast in bed, exotic foods, skin-diving, and water skiing. We were willing to be flexible! Unfortunately, there were no rooms available. No problem. We flipped through the directory and found another fancy beach resort. After making a few more calls and finding all hotels full, Rene took over. He made a few calls and finally secured a hotel for us. We had to sign some papers before a handful of cash was given us. Then Rene took us to a taxi. He was really nice to us those nights at the airport, and I think he even had a good time with us, but I guess he was also kind of glad to get rid of us.

Jeff and I were also glad to be on our way, even if it was our luggage misfortune which made possible this vacation adventure. We were both extremely tired, but enjoying the beautiful ride along the coast. Finally, the taxi pulled up in front of a beautiful Spanish plaza.

Wow! Our missionary trip was getting better! The taxi driver said something briefly in Spanish, pointed toward the plaza and drove off. Although we both just wanted to sleep, we stood in front of the plaza looking at the palm trees, the kids swimming in the ocean, people selling fish on the boardwalk. Well, we thought, there will be time for the skin-diving, skiing and play later. Let's find our way into this big hotel.

"Oh no," I said. I had glanced across the nice plaza, and there was our hotel. It didn't quite go with the plaza, and it was far from being a five-star hotel. When we got into the lobby through the security bars, we could tell that there weren't going to be any water sports, girls with grapes, breakfast in bed and the likes. This was far from being our five-star choice.

The man at the desk didn't speak any words we could understand either. After giving us a key and yapping some quick words at us, he pointed to a gloomy stairway. We went down the dark hall checking for a door our room key might fit. Although the rooms were marked with room numbers, our key wasn't. Finally we found our room.

A few feet further down the hall, the building ceased to exist. It was like a part of the hotel had simply fallen over. The hallway just ended with a two story fall!

Our room was decorated with graffiti and the roaches didn't seem bothered that we had intruded into their territory. We were disappointed, to say the least, but too tired to be upset.

Jeff went into the bathroom to take a shower. It had an electric water heater hanging from the wall. He plugged in the electric shower, sparks flew and smoke came out. While he showered, I attempted to turn the air conditioner on using fingernail clippers since there were no knobs. We were fortunate to have a room with three beds since one was more like a hammock, sagging within a few inches of the floor.

After a few hours sleep, we felt we should let someone know where we were, that we were okay and still on our way. I picked up the phone and started to dial. Some Spanish voice came on and said something I couldn't understand, so I just kept dialing. The operator started yelling at me, and so I just hung up. Jeff and I tried calling a few more times, each time being rudely interrupted. Little did we know one had to give the hotel operator the number, he would dial it and call you back if he got through. We finally gave up and decided to venture out to get something to eat.

We found an uncrowded sidewalk restaurant, but we, not knowing the customs for obtaining service, had problems. Time continued to pass and the waiter continued to ignore us. As we became frustrated, we noticed that those getting service whistled to the waiter much like one would call a dog. We finally got up the nerve and gave a rude whistle; the waiter politely brought us both a menu.

We definitely did not want to look ignorant, but there wasn't a word on the menu that looked familiar to us. No tacos, burritos, no tostadas or enchiladas, not even a hamburger. So, when the waiter returned, we both took turns closing our eyes and pointing at the menu.

We were both pleasantly surprised at the results. We did not know what we were eating, but it didn't matter. The food at the sidewalk restaurants was extremely good except for the roaches that we found in the bottom of the soup dishes. You find them when you are almost finished eating. It's better that way; it doesn't spoil your appetite.

We found ourselves in enough other messes to make it easy for me to temporarily put aside my inner turmoil. After our Caribbean vacation was rudely brought to a close by the arrival of our luggage, Jeff and I had to go into Caracas to take care of some business before proceeding to the jungle. God was teaching us some things for sure. One of our first lessons was learning to understand and appreciate others.

Friendly welcome

Carrying medicines to village

13

A Rude Welcome

Our previous high ideal of what a missionary was would soon be broken. Through it would come a more compassionate understanding, an understanding of what, in part, creates fellow human beings, their character, their person. I understand much better now what makes some missionaries the way they are, since, over the years, I myself have also become a by-product of the same process.

Arriving at the mission apartment in Caracas was a relief. It was much cooler in Caracas than down the mountain where the airport is located. We were welcomed by the director who was friendly and genuinely expressed interest in us and in our work. Another missionary, however, was also passing through the guest home. Although we greeted him, he didn't convey any welcome or greeting to us in return.

Jeff began to unpack some of the bags in back of the apartment while this other missionary looked on. Jeff and I found quite a mess in one of the bags as some excess oil had drained out of the large chain saw we were carrying. The missionary expressed, without a whole lot of tact, that we were just stupid kids and then walked back into the mission apartment. It was obvious that this fellow was not the mission's welcoming committee! Inside the apartment, we could clearly hear him speaking with the director, "I hate short term missionaries. They come and have a good time and when they get tired they go home." Little did this fellow know that we were not having a good time and would not have a good time and he was definitely not the pot of gold at the end of the rainbow.

Although Jeff and I joked about this guy who was so cold toward us, a lingering question of why he acted as he did stuck with us. A few years later, I watched the struggle of life and death in a missionary's hands. Then later I experienced it myself. Then again I went with the others to bury a fellow missionary; since then I have lost other friends, both fellow workers and those I wanted to help. We came to understand a little about this bitterness. Perhaps this bitter missionary had held too many dying Indians in his arms. Perhaps he could not understand any other life outside of the struggle of saving the lives of those with whom he worked and those whom they represent.

What might be considered a "normal" life by most can become distorted in the eyes of some missionaries who kind of lose themselves giving their lives to the people they serve. Perhaps there is little hope for those who do not peek out of the cocoon of their ministry world. After all, what flexibility should anyone expect from someone dealing with constant loneliness, life and death issues, self-worth, isolation and failure? This is especially true when they do finally come back for a break from the mission field and find the opposite extreme almost as frustrating in comparison. What color choir robes? How to finance a new organ? Considerations for a church bell choir?

Shortly after, I suffered the violence, sorrow and

loss of lives in my own corner of service. In part, this matured my understanding of balance between "relativity *of* normality."

As young men, it was difficult for us to see through this missionary's eyes. For him, it could have been very difficult to see why any serious Christian coming to his mission field would ever want to leave. He was, no doubt, overwhelmed with the needs in his corner of the world and to him, we might have looked like a couple of glorified tourists.

This experience opened our eyes to a broader understanding of those on some mission fields who have really become bonded to those they have gone to serve. It later softened our quick judgment of those who seemed to know of no other message than "Go ye." At the time, however, Jeff and I were sure taken back by this guy. As time went on, we felt that although not excusable behavior, we could understand how he might have felt.

A couple of days later, we arrived in a small jungle town. There we purchased our supplies and loaded everything into the small mission plane to head upriver. It was cool flying high above the vast expanse of jungle broken up only by rivers winding their way aimlessly toward the green horizon. We would be in the air for another two hours. A swarm of thoughts buzzed through my mind. No more monkey business, fancy resorts and playing around. It was time to be serious. Jeff and I had heard a lot about this mission base where we would soon land, and it was not good.

Cutting lumber with chainsaw mill, 1980

Jeff during his visit, 1992

14
Snakes and Tarantulas, Ants and Roaches

The small Cessna dropped quickly in over the river, clearing the last bit of jungle before setting down on the short, grass strip. I guess it was just too much too fast, like waking up from a nightmare and finding out that it's not all a dream. The plane was quickly surrounded by half-naked natives. Some laughed as they pointed into the plane. Most kept up a steady rhythm of swatting and slapping the cloud of gnats and mosquitoes.

The pilot swung the door open and immediately a wave of humid heat gushed in. In a few seconds all our exposed skin felt as if hundreds of small needles were being repeatedly poked at us. Every gnat would suck out a drop of blood while leaving another blood drop exposed under the first layer of skin.

We had last seen this missionary from our church at our send-off service dressed in a suit and tie. Now, he didn't look like anyone we had seen before--sick, dirty, skinny, dressed in tattered clothes and soaked from head to foot with sweat. The Indians came over and started feeling the hair on our arms, touching and pulling on our clothes and, generally, giving us a good going over.

I realized that I would face off with God in territory where I had already lost. Old Testament Job desired a judge to mediate between himself and God. I desired no less. I felt hot and faint and the hundreds of bites had my face, neck and arms swelling. I excused myself and walked away from everyone to the edge of the river.

There I prayed the first prayer in months that had made it further than a stone's throw. I was sincere, not real spiritual, very honest, but feeling already defeated.

"Dear Lord," I prayed, "here I will die. I just hope that wherever I am going is better than this."

I sat staring for a moment at the river. The moment I took to quit swatting the gnats was enough time for them to get into my eyes and nose. I quickly stood up and made my way back up the slippery bank. The plane took off.

The Indians helped carry our bags to a mud and pole structure with a thatched roof. There we hung our hammocks while the Indians commented on everything we had in our bags. Our accommodations were simple. A hammock to sleep in and a cut-off tree stump for each of us to put a few items on off the mud floor.

It took a few nights to get used to our living routine. All night long the roof sounded like a candy wrapper being crumpled as thousands of roaches covering the inside of our roof went about their business. It took a little getting used to, having the roaches lose their footing from time to time falling on top of us at night. With practice I perfected quickly picking the stray roach off my body and tossing it to the floor without smashing it on my chest or dramatically disturbing my sleep.

It was best to keep personal items, toothbrushes and small things in a plastic bag hung from a string to keep the roaches, leaf cutter ants or rats from chewing on them or carrying them away. The roaches would chew around the edges of almost anything. The leaf-cutter ants had to be watched for at night. They would come by the thousands taking anything in their path. The rats were just a bother. At night they liked running down our hammock ropes into our hammocks.

We never had much luck trying to shoot the rats out of the roof, but we did develop a highly competitive roach killing tournament. If both Jeff and I felt relatively okay health-wise, we would take our shoes and set them in different spots around the room in the early evening. At night we would take turns, one holding a flashlight, the other ready to run to any shoe in the room when the light was turned on. The objective was to smash with the shoes as many roaches as possible on the wall or floor before they would run under the walls or into the roof. Each smashed roach was worth one point. The ants would carry off all the dead roaches before the next night, leaving a clean slate for a new competition.

Much of the time there was an atmosphere of tension. The missionary family was living in a part of the village loaned them by the Indians. Life was hard, especially for the wife who struggled against all odds to cook meals, carry water from the river, care for the sick children and her husband who was sick much of the time as well.

Fights broke out in the village all too often. One night Jeff and I were visiting with some of the Indian men on one side of the village when screams rang out, echoing through the jungle. One of the men, who is still a good friend today, called one of the others to settle a dispute. As he ducked through the opening, he was attacked and his head was laid wide open with an ax. It started a pole fight in the dark. Men ran in with machetes, axes, arrows and poles. We were hit as we ducked for cover.

We quickly learned to keep proper composure at difficult times. Being only 18 years old at the time, it was difficult for us to estimate and calculate all of the risks and dangers. We had not been in the village more than a couple of weeks when a war was about to break out on the other side of the river.

Jeff and I reluctantly followed instructions from the veteran missionary who told us to run into the jungle. He said we would find men hiding with their bows and arrows.

When things heat up, some will want to shoot. Stand in front of them. That we did. It was a bit unnerving, looking down a pointed arrow shaft into the angry eyes of a painted warrior; however, an all out battle was prevented.

Early one morning, while it was still dark, our missionary friend woke us, screaming for help.

"They are killing a girl at the end of the village," he yelled, and then he disappeared into the darkness. Jeff and I jumped up out of our hammocks and ran out. We couldn't see much as we ran to the other side of the village, but the yelling and screaming got louder as we approached. We arrived at the outside edge of the group not knowing what to do. There were men and women from another village all painted up, some wielding machetes, others arrows.

Finally we spotted our friend in the middle of a group of fighting Indians with a teenage girl being pulled from side to side as the two groups fought over her. We could see that the girl was already in bad shape. They had tried to hack her up with their machetes. They were trying to take her back from our villagers who were trying to protect her. Jeff and I forcefully fought our way through the crowd to the girl.

The missionary yelled for us to help them get the girl out of the crowd to safety, since they were still hacking at her with machetes. Jeff and I started pushing the enemy men back, but when we did, we were met with greater opposition. We just did as we were told, although we weren't sure of the wisdom of these instructions. Jeff went into his high school football mode and started dumping the enemy men back into the jungle undergrowth. We fought for a time with the friendly Indians at our side until a break opened and they ran off to protect and hide the girl. The two villages continued fighting each other with machetes. It was a mess; some people were badly hurt. There were men and women alike with machete gashes across their faces, heads and arms.

Suddenly one of the enemy men angrily ran out with a shotgun he had grabbed from somewhere. The missionary waved desperately for me to take it from him. I ran by, grabbing it from the painted warrior. Two Indians with machetes took off after me and Jeff after them. Jeff tackled one who fell on his own machete cutting his hand wide open. Things remained tense with the fighting lasting into the late morning. We received a crash course in giving first aid.

Jeff and I found life there to be difficult and trying more than challenging and interesting. We had to grow up quickly. We had to fight to survive. Many similar experiences, violence, tension, hardships worked together molding our views, perspectives and lives.

Our work was not easy. That particular year, the heat and insects were worse than usual. We would get up while it was still dark, walk down the trail to the dugout canoe and motor our way up river to the trail that led to where we were cutting lumber. Just as Jeff and I would arrive at the logs we had sectioned for milling, there would be enough light in the sky to begin work. The work was hard and heavy and left us exhausted every day. The heat and biting insects were almost unbearable. Some mornings, the temperature would reach 110 degrees before nine o'clock.

I was still struggling with everything inside. Apart from the constant stresses in the village, most mornings we would not only have to battle the heat and bugs but also the poisonous snakes and tarantulas that found comfortable shelter under our equipment cover at night.

Jeff and I were sick most of the time. Every few days one or both of us would experience intense intestinal pains and vomiting. Our work would stop for a few minutes until we regained our composure. Jeff contracted some fungus which caused his hands and feet to crack and constantly bleed. I was ill, too. There were times when going to relieve myself, all that would come out were balls of tangled worms. Jeff lost a lot of weight. Many times after our night meal, if we had one, one or both of us would throw it up before the night was through. We both battled through sickness week after week, month after month. Even in all our sickness we did not stop working although it made everything all the more difficult.

Villages at war, 1980

Alto Ocamo, 1992-1993

15

Still Sick, But Set Free

One day we were cutting trees on a steep jungle slope. Almost a dozen trees had been cut but had not fallen due to the many vines holding them all together. I planted my feet into the hillside to cut the tree that apparently was holding the others from coming down. When the trees started to fall, I pulled the chain saw from the tree. At the same time, the ground gave way below me and I fell, the running chain saw falling on top of my leg. Blood was everywhere.

The Indians got real nervous seeing all the blood. Thankfully, it wasn't that bad. When the Indians saw that it wasn't life threatening they were quite amused by the whole event.

Time went on. Jeff and I brought poles and the lumber we had cut down the river for building homes for the two missionary families. We enjoyed working with the Indians and learned a lot from them during our months there in the jungle.

One morning, I woke up very sick. I was shaking, in a cold sweat. I quickly got worse. High fevers left me delirious. When I opened my eyes, everything around me spun in circles. I knew enough to realize that if I got much worse my problems would be permanently solved. As the days went by, some of the Indians would quietly come in during the day and look at me for a minute then leave. The roaches continued to fall into my hammock from the roof, but I no longer cared. As close as I felt to dying, it wasn't yet my time to go.

Time passed and I was able to get back on my feet again. I started to wonder why I had not died, and at the same time, I was not very encouraged that I hadn't. As the days continued to slip by, the nagging possibility of my not dying became a worse nightmare. I was still sick, discouraged, angry at God and not finding any solution to the many questions that followed me day and night. Now a new problem presented itself; what if I don't die here and God doesn't do anything to heal me?

I had very little desire to live. My previous idea of God's intervention, healing and restoration had been totally scrapped. How could I be so bitter at the age of eighteen?

I went back through the Scriptures, each night reading by candle-light in my hammock. I wanted to come to some absolute conclusion and either find a miracle or forget about God altogether. For whatever reason, things started to find new meaning. There were battles with God over parts of His Word I could not reconcile. There were nights when I blew out my candle and just lay quietly for hours. Distant lightning would illuminate the surrounding jungle for a fraction of a second while the thunder echoed through my empty soul.

Many conflicts were not resolved; however, one night, my life changed. Something happened that night which would change my life forever. No angel in shining white robes, no flashing lights, no voice from heaven and there was no great supernatural experience. Nevertheless, there was a surrender that night which set me free.

There were a number of things that had boiled out of my struggle with God and His Word. One was that although I had trusted in Jesus, it was in a way perhaps better related to Old Testament Cain. Yes, I had believed, but my confidence was more set in my belief and in my faith than in whom I was putting that faith. God had to be conformed to my ideas of how He should act. Therefore, like Cain, the only thing I could offer God was my best. For what more could God ask? He would be unfair to ask for more than a person has. That was the premise from which Cain's failure came. Like Cain, I felt I deserved better. Cain was more spiritual than his brother Abel, for it was Cain who first brought an offering to the Lord. God looked favorably upon Abel and upon his offering, but not on Cain or his offering.

Although I had grown up understanding and believing that the basis of salvation is by faith alone, it was *my* faith, *my* way, that created a foundational problem seated in self. God had given Cain an opportunity to change his way of seeing things, but he opted out. If there was any doubt to the nature of Cain's offering being one of ego, it should be removed a couple verses later when religious Cain, the first to bring an offering to God, raises up and murders his brother.

The foundational difference between Cain and Abel is perhaps more clearly seen if we extend their two shadows towards the cross where Jesus is crucified. There we find two criminals being crucified, one on each side of Jesus. Do you see the likeness of Cain and Abel here? The Lamb of God, sacrificed, shedding innocent blood, separates the two guilty men. One despises him, the other finds his faith entwined in the sacrifice and blood of Jesus in whom he has all his hope. There are two precepts here that glare out from the beginning of the Bible and become louder as the story approaches Jesus Christ.

Although I had "become a Christian" at the age of eleven according to all the traditional standards, that night in the jungle was for me a new birth. I had sincerely done all the other stuff; I had raised my hand when the invitation to receive Christ was given. I had repeated the prescribed traditional prayer. I had been to plenty of meetings where it seemed like the call to "receive Christ" was kind of like being conned into buying some kind of fancy soap.

Most of what I had gleaned from a lot of this evangelism stuff growing up was that one needed to "accept God." He would help you with all your problems and help you be a better person. In return, you would try to be a good Christian, do your best, give God your best effort.

Well God didn't seem interested in helping me with my problems and making me a better person. And my best effort? Big deal. Who cares about my best effort? God didn't need my best effort nor will my best effort ever be worth anything to anyone, anywhere at any time.

Although I was serving Him, sacrificing for Him, working for Him and even dying for His work in that forsaken swamp in the middle of the disease-ridden jungle, everything had its central control in my hands.

All was silent. In the dark I prayed and for the first time in my life, the burdens and weight fell from my shoulders. I put my faith in action. That action was getting out of the driver's seat of my life.

"God, I don't understand why you have allowed all this sickness, why my prayers seem to have had no answers, why all the endless feeling of loneliness, but I do believe You. No matter what happens, I'm Yours."

This unimpressive prayer didn't bring an end to my afflictions, for most continued on for years. That dark night in the Amazon was a culmination of months of spiritual wrestling which left me with some perspectives of life which have very much been a blessing to me over these years.

God was certainly not interested in convincing me to be a missionary. We both knew that he didn't and doesn't need me to do any of His work. I think a lot of Christians feel that way. Perhaps many would say "amen" to that, although it is sad that for many this truth only serves to delude life's values, reducing life's purpose to a pursuit of personal comfort, self-gratification, self-centered activities and lifestyle choices.

This ends up being a sad and empty existence. God certainly isn't interested in our seeking fulfillment in building our own little kingdoms during this fleeting life. Neither has He called us to give ourselves to pursuing happiness. As for me, I believe my living precepts were more tied to Cain, even though I was already a "Christian" at the time. Although a lot of nice things might come out of "Cainness," God was patiently prodding me towards Abel.

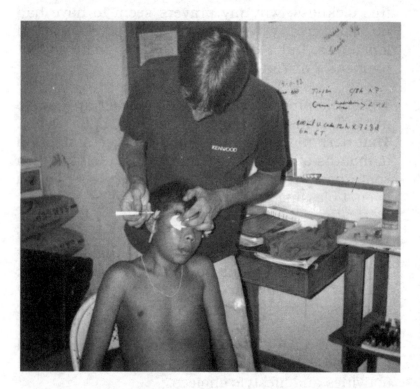

Rick suturing a cut

16

God's Way

A part of the Gospel of Mark made this point clearer to me during those challenging months and years. It made me take a hard look at my own failing life and a careful look at what contributed to my mistaken precepts.

Jesus had been teaching his disciples. Now the time arrived that He would teach them clearly that He would suffer great pain, that He would be rejected by society's political and spiritual leaders, that He would be killed and that three days later He would be resurrected. I can't imagine the impact this must have made on the men who left everything to follow him. Perhaps the part about being resurrected slipped by His disciples.

Either way, the disciples loved Jesus. Peter loved him very much. It was Peter who took Jesus aside and began to rebuke Him. We can only guess what was said in this brief counseling time. But, there is one thing we know for sure: Peter's attitude reflects the attitude of many of us and our churches today!   And so Peter is rebuked by Jesus, in front of everyone.

The reason for Jesus' sternly rebuking Peter, "You, Peter, have your mind set on man's ways, not on God's." In those few words Jesus sums up what has been an on-going struggle since Adam and Eve, man's ways versus God's ways. We can hardly deny it. Let's not get our feelings hurt, but look at what it has slowly produced. Since Adam pointed his finger at Eve, and Eve at Satan, we have no one to point at but ourselves. I know I'm sticking my neck out on this, but this is only a part of the sum-total of man's ways, not God's.

Let's consider a couple of related points. Much of our going to church today is just that, *going* to church, not *being* the church. Are we satisfied with a two-hour a week participation at "being" the body of Christ? We ask our congregations to give "unto the Lord" so that we can build bigger and nicer church buildings for our own enjoyment, buy new choir robes, carpet or bells for a bell choir. Can you imagine Jesus or any of His disciples standing before the hungry crowds ringing bells?

There is nothing wrong with nice buildings, new choir robes, carpet or bells. What might be called into question, however, is the motive of our vast spending on these things or the collective values these pursuits reveal. What is the vision that overwhelmingly represents our time, attention and resources as a church?

Can you imagine what an impact a church would have in its community if it took the same hours it spent on last year's Christmas cantata and this year spend the time simply sweeping the streets of the neighborhood and helping out at an elderly widow's home? Without a single tract passed out, door bell rung or having to suspend poor little Johnny from the sanctuary rafters with aluminum foil angel wings, a community could see some of the practical application of Christian care. In many or most cases, we have found a "better way" than what Jesus said, "Go and make disciples." We don't need to go anywhere. We just need to have an attractive enough program to induce folks to attend some church meeting. If the preacher or pastor is a good enough speaker, he may be able to convince some of the attendees to "believe in Jesus."

Believe in Jesus? Believe what about Jesus? A wonderful short cut; man's ways aren't so bad after all!

So much of our confusion is a result of the great void which lies between the best of our spiritual reasoning and the simple words of Jesus, "God's way."

In perhaps one of the most intense moments of the short years of Jesus' ministry on this earth, He rebukes Peter. You can feel the tension as Jesus turns to call His other disciples near.   He also beckons to the multitude beyond them. The people began to gather around. Peter, was probably still in a daze over Jesus' response; after all, he was only trying to help! The other disciples must have been wondering as well. As the people gathered around, Jesus began to speak.

"If anyone wishes to come after Me, let him deny himself, take up his cross and follow Me. For whoever wants to save his life will lose it, but whoever loses his life for me and for the Gospel will save it."   Mark 8:34-35

Our brand of faith today has lost much of that driving and separating force. These words demanded more from those listening than those who were called by Moses after the Israelites had turned away from God to worship a golden calf.

Moses saw that the people were running wild and that Aaron had let them get out of control, becoming a laughing stock to their enemies. So he stood at the entrance to the camp and said, *"Whoever is for the Lord, come to me."* (Exodus 32:25-26)

Moses had found the Israelites worshipping a calf after committing themselves wholly to God. It was time to separate the real fruit from the artificial. No one was to be left in the middle. It was one or the other.

What would be the outcome if this scene were to be repeated today? What would be the response to Jesus? Jesus wouldn't have a chance in many of our churches today. Jesus would not be chosen by the pastor selection committee. He would not last because of his "terrible testimony."

You can hear the talk, "How dare this man get up in church and cause such a division. He tried to cut most of us down to nothing with his indirect comments. He certainly has no room to talk. Have you seen the people he associates with? He never has time to participate in the church growth programs or the committee planning meetings or choir, and he hasn't participated even once in the sanctuary pulpit decoration rotation. He is always with his sinner friends!"

But these words of Jesus were not another altar call for everyone to finally come forward on the last stanza of "Just As I Am." This was no call to believe in Jesus *per se*. It is interesting how we define someone getting "saved" in contrast to the various ways we find people "saved" in the New Testament. Paul, for one example, never "prayed to receive Christ," nor did he follow the "four spiritual laws," nor did he raise his hand or "go forward." He demonstrated a turn of heart which reflected his new found faith. His life became conformed to the life of Jesus.

Child was saved by medicine provided by IAM partners – malaria epidemic, 1992

Film translation project, 1990
Villagers view Gospel film for first time

17

If Anyone Wishes to Come....

A choice, an intersection in the road, a decision.

"If anyone wishes to come after me." This was the establishing of a foundation of conditions which greatly contrasted Peter's "man's way" counsel to Jesus. Jesus laid before the crowd three conditions. As I considered the meaning of these in my own life over the past years, I found that the more I grow in Him, the more I actually fail in these three areas.

The three conditions are evolutionary in their application. What I need to work on today may not be my need tomorrow. Nevertheless, if we are not honest with ourselves in considering the revolutionary effects of this call, we are bound to continue on in a Christianity very much adjusted, adapted, custom tailored and fluffed up to our own liking. A nice faith for sure but not a real one. Before briefly considering these conditions, I need to say for the sake of anyone seriously considering these thoughts, God judges the heart. We are better off being humble before God's Word, especially when we don't understand the situations or circumstances in which we find ourselves.

"The heart is deceitful above all things and beyond cure. Who can understand it? I, the Lord, search the heart and examine the mind...." (Jeremiah 17:9-10). The moment we look at ourselves too introspectively, either we are bound to form a better concept of how we are doing

than how we really are, or we judge ourselves more harshly than God would.

It is safe to say that in our daily living we will find dramatic changes in lifestyle, direction, character and activity as we consider these conditions Jesus laid down for his followers in light of His claims on our lives.

"If anyone wishes to come after Me, let him":
(1) *Deny himself.* It is not enough that we just serve God. Such service can come from the principle Cain established, "I will offer to God what is appropriate in my sight. God should be pleased with whatever His children offer Him." How nice this would be, each one doing as he or she sees best.

In 1 Samuel 15:20-23, Saul feels that he did better than just obeying the Lord. The Lord had commanded that Saul destroy his enemies and all their possessions. Saul felt that he had done better in taking the king prisoner and saving the best of the animals for a sacrifice unto the Lord, in the Lord's honor. Read the story for yourself. Saul lost his reign over Israel not because he failed to serve the Lord but because he adjusted his service to his own way, not God's. The consequences of his sin were passed on.

Deny self? Self is everything that befriends death. Yes, it was self and pride which extended Eve's hand to take of disobedience. Self feeds pride and pride turned to anger in Cain. He disobeyed also and, in anger, killed his brother. As history continues, so self-centered interests multiplied. All this being said does not mean that Christ had the idea that we should torture ourselves and do everything possible to make ourselves unhappy. Rather, he was calling us to a better standard. He expected us to put others first, to count others as more important than ourselves, to seek the good of others over ourselves! A tough challenge for us in an age of competition, self-centered goals and pursuits.

(2) *Take up his cross.* An interesting thing for Jesus to say. How is it that He would tell those listening to take up their cross knowing that He would not only take up their cross but would die on it. I have often meditated on this principle of substitution. Throughout the Old Testament we see incredible reflections of that which was to come in Christ. In the account of Abraham and Isaac (Genesis 22), God provided a substitute sacrifice to take Isaac's place. In the Passover (Exodus 12), the sign of the blood would cause the judgement to pass over. Those behind the door were covered, nothing else would be considered.

So here we have Jesus inviting others to come take up their cross. In the context, we find it to be a decision to side one way or the other. But he who wishes to save his life shall lose it. Whoever loses his life for Jesus and the Gospel will save it. Paul later portrays this as a death to self that his vessel might be consumed by Christ.

Jesus took up our cross of sin that you and I would not have to pay for that sin. Jesus, as our substitute lamb, shed His blood on the frame of that cross, just as the blood of the lamb was the protection for those behind the door frames in Egypt that you and I may be free; even free to take up a cross.

Perhaps we lift the burden of another that his eyes would see Jesus. Perhaps, as His spirit leads us, we would bear another's burden. Just as someone came along in our time of need and led us to see Him who saves, we would do the same for others. Such actions, however, can be costly. The cross was costly. What it paid for was life. Life was given that life might be received. Jesus gave His life, not only that we would be saved but that we might also receive His life as our own.

(3) *Follow Me*. What does it mean to follow Christ? This could be a difficult venture for us not understanding the task. Even the disciples didn't get it right. After Jesus stood in the storm and rebuked the wind and waves, He then turned to His disciples and asked, *"Where is your faith? How is it you have no faith?"* (Luke 8:22-25).

In Mark 6, Jesus does a miracle in feeding thousands of people from five pieces of bread and two fish. In chapter 8, he feeds thousands more by multiplying seven loaves of bread. A short time after, they are traveling in a boat and the disciples start discussing how short they are on food. Can you imagine being in the same boat with Him who fed thousands from virtually nothing? Jesus says to them, *"Why do you discuss the fact that you have no bread? Do you not yet see or understand?"*

He reminds them of what was collected after He had fed the multitudes both times and then asks again, *"Do you not yet understand?"*

Following Christ is much more a disposition of heart. It's not where you go for Christ, but where you are in Christ. So many times, when someone mentions the phrase "following Christ," right away we think, "Oh no, not another one of those missionaries. They are always pushing for people to go to Africa and places like that." Not so, Jesus may not send you to Africa, but, rather, to another field of service, your own home!

In Luke 8, Jesus heals a demon-possessed man. As Jesus moves on, the man begs Jesus that he might accompany Him, but Jesus sends him away: *"Return to your house and describe what great things God has done for you."* That he did!

When Jesus said, "Follow Me," He was inviting the multitude to start a life of faith, to walk by faith, to live by faith and to finish by faith.

All these and other considerations flowed together. This was a pivotal point. After praying, I blew out my candle. I did not fall asleep right away. However, for the first time in a long time I was at peace. The sicknesses didn't all go away. In fact, it got worse, but my spirit was at peace.

Discipleship team training in desert, 1985

18
The Death of Casper's Father

Months turned to years and I was still very sick. The United States government tropical disease laboratory in Panama accepted me as a case study. When I first entered this lab, I felt certain I was in the wrong place. I walked between rows of cages containing monkeys and other animals, but no, it was the right place. The laboratory testing was done at no cost to me since it was a research lab. I was just another monkey to study!

As the years passed, I finally got over some of my health problems. I grew in God's grace while He opened new doors and vision.

In 1983, I led the first team of what would become a yearly discipleship program. International Youth Missions was born. I had two young men in that first group and never took more than four men in any one team.

Each team joined me for an intense three-month discipleship experience. They lived with me in Mexico, working and serving among the poor. Language study and culture study, ministry and learning humility within the context of poor communities south of the U.S.-Mexican border constituted the first phase. This was followed by a boot camp in the hot, desolate Southern California desert, providing a time of team growth, practical study and training. There in the desert, each of us learned to depend on the other team members. Following the desert, we traveled to the mountains for a jungle training camp which entailed training for tasks to be done on a South American field, as well as teaching on relationships, servanthood, team work and missions.

After completing these three phases, I led the teams to South America. Over the years, with the Indian groups involved, we built numerous missionary homes, clinics and schools. The goal was not constructing buildings but building lives. Our work simply earned us the privilege of learning on the field.

God used the discipleship program to lead team members in different directions. Although the goal wasn't for them to sign up for any particular ministry or mission, more than half of the guys are now actively involved in ministry, some as missionaries on foreign fields. The teams worked very hard and some under dangerous circumstances. Living conditions were very basic and primitive.

I probably learned at least as much as I taught, and God used my team members to affect my own life through our living and working together. A book could be written on the experiences from Mexico to the desert to the Amazon. God worked in special and significant ways in each of our lives.

God used others along the way to teach me. Upon completing training in our discipleship each year and after sending my groups back to North America, I would return up-river to the Yanomamö people. I couldn't stay more than an additional month or so, as I had to get back to work and the business of supporting myself and the work in Mexico. But my time up-river lent to further ministry opportunities and personal growth. Not all my experiences were gratifying, but all were building blocks in my life.

One sad event I shared with a missionary friend of mine who lives in the Amazon. I have known Mike for many years. He is close to the Indians and spends a lot of time with them. I've had the privilege of working with Mike and have been both encouraged and challenged by his faithfulness.

In 1980, prior to meeting Mike, Jeff and I worked with the Yanomamö in building the house which would be home for a family being sent out from our own church in San Diego. At that time we met some Yanomamö from up-river. One of the men we met from an up-river village became a special friend.

Jeff and I named this man Casper for his blue-green eyes, a characteristic which is an exception within his ethnic group. We spent much time with Casper working in the jungle and on the trail and river. Although I had never visited his village—up two rivers and a hike through the jungle—, I would someday have that opportunity.

The missionary family from our church moved in and began work, but the constant battle with disease, infection and sickness took its toll. It wasn't long before the wife became sick and her life was saved only by a last minute primitive tracheotomy done by Mike's brother. Her windpipe was slit open in the village and her life was saved in a desperate operation. Treatment for her infirmities was a drawn out ordeal after being flown to a U.S. hospital. They never returned to the field.

In the jungle, sickness can come suddenly and, at times, with considerable consequence. Malaria is most often the villain. The sorrow of failed attempts to save lives can be difficult to describe. Late one afternoon, just before nightfall, a voice echoed through the jungle from across the river. A couple of Yanomamö men paddled over to where they found the man who was calling. It was Casper. He had run hard all day through the jungle, his body was torn by thorns; he was hungry and exhausted. He shook as he explained his mission.

"My father was in the garden yesterday when he fell to the ground shaking. The other men there saw my father being attacked by the spirits. They quickly started to strangle him to kill the spirits. I pushed them away and picked up my father, carrying him back to the village. I stayed with him all night, and early this morning I started to run. Please help my father," Casper pleaded.

By now it was already dark. Casper had run a long distance. He had seen the effects of medicine and hoped that we could help. That night, we filled a backpack with medical supplies and some rice and by moonlight filled gas tanks for the trip up-river. Before light the next morning, Mike and I and several Yanomamö men, including Casper, walked down the muddy bank to the canoe, already loaded and ready. Shortly after departing, there was enough light to make out the edge of the jungle through the thick fog. Nobody spoke as we sped upriver through the darkness and fog.

When we got to the trail, Casper led the way. I followed with Mike and the others. Casper kept a quick pace as we trudged through mud, waded through streams and pushed through the thick undergrowth. We crossed ravines on simple bridges made of one or two poles. While crossing one of these bridges, the narrow pole bridge broke as I neared the middle. A sharp pain pierced my ribs as I fell through the limbs of a tree below and finally to the ground.

Keeping up with Casper was a task. As the hours passed, I continued thinking about Casper's father. Casper walked faster and faster, his concern obvious. The heat and humidity pushed down heavily upon us, as well as the anticipation of what we might be able to do, if anything at all. Finally the trail became more than just a few marked trees and I knew we were getting close. Casper disappeared down the trail. I continued as quickly as I could until I heard a distant scream. I stopped on the trail to listen.

Off in the distance echoed more screams and death wails. I dropped my pack to the ground and along with it the hope of finding Casper's father alive. I sat on the trail and stared at the ground as sweat continued to pour down my face, back and chest. Soon a couple of the Yanomamö caught up. I looked up at them; their faces were stern and serious. To them it was a fatalistic, sad and angry moment. They quickly laid down their bows and arrows and began to smear black dye over their bodies. When everyone was suitably painted, we continued on through the jungle to the village clearing.

When we came to the outer part of the village, the men with us joined the villagers. Men danced back and forth with their bows and arrows, women with sharpened poles and machetes. Around the hammock where Casper's father lay, some of the Yanomamö were beating on the poles to which his hammock was tied. The village rang with screams and wailing. The structure shook as the mourners beat against the pole supports.

Mike leaned over and asked, "Is the hammock shaking from everyone pounding on the poles or is Casper's father moving?" I couldn't tell. We walked through the crowd of wailing men and women to his hammock. We reached out and touched his body. He was alive! Although unconscious and twisted from violent convulsions, he was breathing. The people gathered around and it became very quiet except for a few who continued crying.

They were afraid to touch him for fear of the spirits.

We asked for water to wash him off and try to lower the fever. He was severely dehydrated.

Dried vomit covered his neck and chest; violent convulsions wrenched it out of him. His hammock was soaked with other body fluids from the attacks. He would lay deathly still for a few minutes and then convulse violently.

He was worse than others I've seen in similar stages, some choking with intestinal worms crawling up their throat and out their nose or mouth. Mike continued bathing him down; I prepared the first injection. As I drew back the solution, I looked up into the many faces surrounding us, but quickly looked back down.

Every eye held that question, "You are going to save him, aren't you?" I wasn't that optimistic; neither was Mike.

We worked with him until after dark and in a few hours he seemed to be a bit improved although still unconscious. Every hour or so one of us got up to check on him. Another injection, more time cooling the high fever. The screams subsided and some went to lie in their hammocks; others squatted in a circle around him.

At one point, Mike came back to where we had our hammocks hung and said excitedly, "I think he is getting better!   Half conscious, he said 'Ya amishi, ya amishi' (I'm thirsty, I'm thirsty)." Mike was able to get several spoonfuls of water into his mouth. Our hope mounted. We prayed.

The village remained quiet. Perhaps everything would work out. We were encouraged that all the thinking, praying, walking and the hours next to his hammock might have a happy end. Just before dawn, however, we woke to more screams and soon the entire village was in an uproar. Casper's father had passed into eternity. Someone started chopping firewood and preparing a pile in the middle of the clearing to burn the body. Rain started to pour. In the middle of the village I watched Casper. He danced back and forth with his arrows overhead. His tears fell to the ground with the rain.

Some of the village men came and told us that we could go. It was over. We took down our hammocks and walked out into the rain. The villagers were dancing, wailing, screaming. We were quietly defeated. Casper came over to us as we prepared to walk back into the jungle. He didn't say much. He said their equivalent of good-bye, and, as he looked into our eyes, his own again poured rivers of grief.

We walked away from the village. At the edge of the jungle I turned for a moment. The rain sounded like a waterfall as it fell through the heavy jungle foliage, but it did little to drown out the screams of our friends in that dark village. I wiped the rain from my face to see them once more. The last sight that day would not be easily forgotten, a great multitude in despair. I turned and walked into the dark jungle. Soon the wails and screams melted away into the sound of the falling rain.

In the years to come, I would return to these trails

of such grief carved deeply into other faces, in other places. Perhaps those of the Amazon are more vivid because while being in Mexico, the experiences of South America seem so far away. I see them at night; I can hear the screams when I close my eyes. Those furthest upriver are worlds away from here. I pray for them daily and wish I could reach them. While in the jungle I have many of the same thoughts about those I know back in Mexico.

It has been a great blessing from God to live and work with Indian friends and missionaries in the Amazon basin. God's first call on me, however, was to the poor in Mexico. To Mexico my sights would have to be focused, even though many faces from the rain forests are also engraved into my mind. I was young and could not imagine how much both South America and Mexico would become part of my life.

Trip back upriver, 2001

Discipleship team devotional in Indian village

Discipleship teams work alongside Indians

19

Rice Christians and Rice Missions

As the years passed, I continued supporting myself by working in the construction trade while also studying part-time at a community college and working in Mexico. For awhile, I worked at the Mexican municipal trash dump where Pastor Von had begun helping the people on his day off each week. The people there were truly a needy, hurting people. In many ways, they were friendly towards us and welcomed our visits each week. Violent things happened at the dump, mostly at night.

The homes were simple. Cardboard, tacked-on plastic, a scrap of board, an old car hood for one wall, all wrapped with wire to hold it together, and a couple of tires on top to keep the roof from blowing away. Few homes had outhouses. Fewer still had a septic hole dug underneath. It didn't matter; everything flowed together into the dump.

The families there worked hard; at least until many well-intentioned Christian groups corrupted the dump with a mix of evangelism and welfare. As more and more groups began visiting the dump, some residents found it all too simple to just quit working altogether. The compassionate Christian visitors gave away so much stuff that the dump people could earn plenty a couple days a week in selling the American mercy gifts at swap meets. The weekends would be dedicated to "being poor" and receiving more goods from the generous Christian groups, a couple of days could be given to selling those gifts and the rest of the time, well, that's another story.

In the early days, the people dug through the tons of trash arriving daily. First, any food still edible was picked out, then the long process of extracting treasures. A treasure was anything that had any value in itself, broken things that could be converted to useful things. A broken toy cart together with a bicycle tire rim, a piece of pipe and a broken shopping cart could be fashioned into a wheelbarrow of sorts! Then glass and metal were extracted to form piles weighing tons. This in turn was sold and the little profit yielded sustained the dump community.

Later I worked there with another missionary. He worked with the men of the community, joining them side by side in their struggle. A number of community development projects were carried out. My friend, Andres, had the confidence of the men, but making headway was difficult. For whatever reason, this missionary finally had a nervous breakdown, ending his work there.

Things happened at the dump that perhaps twisted our views of "normal" living. Abused children, children who disappear, murder, rape, death and oppression were facts of life in the dump. I remember one day one of my friends there called to me in a very aggravated tone. He was the head of one of the few homes that boasted a real family unit (a "husband" and "wife" and the children all from that relationship).   As I approached, I saw tears in his eyes.

He cried out in anger, "We are not dogs," he motioned for me to follow him. We ducked through the low entrance of his cardboard home.

"Look what my children found in the trash today," he said. There on the floor were several aborted babies. A pile of them had been dumped "in our neighborhood," my friend cried. And, to add insult to injury, for a joke, a few more fetuses had been thrown in front of this man's humble home.

Life went on for good or for bad there. Many American Christian and secular groups found it a fantastic adventure "helping the dump people." It was their "help" which made real ministry there difficult; the community had learned a new, "adjusted" lifestyle.

During the week the people would joke about "Los Evangélicos," the evangelicals, who would come without fail every Saturday. They came with food and clothing and other gifts. The poorer that one appeared, the more he would be rewarded. And so it went; most every weekend, vans and buses and trailers would pull in over the hill to "help the dump people." With cameras flashing, food and clothing were passed out. "Rice missions" produce "rice Christians."

A few groups worked hard to really help those who needed assistance. They did all they could do to maintain the dignity of the people. These were very few and they could not hold back the tide of the multitude of groups which naively believe that Mexico can be evangelized with no more than a handful of Spanish tracts or a film and a bag of beans or rice. However, what they saw was convincing enough to them. I guess we just watched from a different perspective.

Week after week, the same people would "get saved" and be rewarded or "blessed" with some beans or rice or some other token expressing thanks for their response to the message. In time, the people learned that poverty was their most valuable resource. The worse you looked, the more you would be given.

Many groups walked around like tourists in a zoo. Some would gawk and hold their noses while others clicked off photo after photo. Some groups would stand on top of their bus or van and throw food and clothing into the unruly crowd. As the people fought over the nicer items, they were photographed. In later years, some of those in the dump learned to charge for their photo. There are endless stories best left behind in that smoldering dump along with the piles of burning dogs, the aborted babies, the trash and the corruptions left by many well-meaning ministries.

Christian missions could learn a lot from the dump. Much would depend on the vantage point, I suppose. Evangelism without teaching and discipleship can be a disaster. It's happened many times. A great deal of harm and destruction can be caused by "the ministry." The sad thing is the "evangelist" may be the last to ever realize what has been done. Another sad reality is that although Tijuana boasts of many strong Mexican churches, in the years we frequented the dump, we never saw a Mexican church attempting any ministry there. Those most capable of meeting most of the real needs would not mix with these people of the dump. I do believe that God could have done a real great work there if some, or at least one Mexican church would have really gotten involved, really taught and discipled the people. The ministry they needed the most and those most capable of really helping them never quite arrived.

The dump ended up being a fairly hopeless place to minister. In my personal opinion, in many ways, "missions" made it so.

Grupo Mexico flooded during rains

**Some of these children died in a house fire
shortly after this was taken**

**Dave Burdette building small homes using
his dismantled "haunted house," 1985**

20

A Thanksgiving Meal

Maria is a common but sacred name in Mexico. Maria is also a dedicated, strong and, for the most part, fearless Christian girl. Although she would not boast these qualities herself, this was the Maria whom I got to know early on. I sometimes accompanied her on her personal ministry visits into some rough settlements in canyons on the outskirts of Tijuana. There are too few Christian missionary women like Maria. I had the privilege of working with her for more than six years. She is a Godly woman, dedicated to seeing others brought under the grace of God. In late 1985, Maria told me about a community springing up not far from the dump. Another missionary friend, Dave, had discovered this new settlement. If anyone could turn darkness to light, it was Dave.

Dave has always been appreciated by those with whom he ministers. He works hard to help others and demonstrates genuine concern for them. Dave was battling with many of the same struggles I was confronting at the time, balancing a growing ministry with earning a living.

During this time he was building small homes in Tijuana for destitute families. He had received the donation of a large dismantled Halloween haunted house. You could tell where Dave had been building in this new area. One just needed to look for the black houses with grave stones, ghosts or skeletons painted all over them. It was through Dave and his haunted house that God opened the door for the eventual planting of the community's first church.

Our little team worked together over the years in Grupo Mexico. Juan was there from the beginning. He later married one of the girls from the Grupo Mexico church. He and his wife, Cristina, have a strong gift for working with children and youth among other things. Actually I knew Juan some ten years prior to our starting the work in Grupo Mexico. He has been a dedicated, sacrificial, hard worker and good friend. Juan served the church through some very difficult times. He was assaulted numerous times, once during a church service. I appreciate him and his faithfulness over all the years. I've met few men like him. Years later, Juan became the new director of the drug rehabilitation program and developed a work with a lot of the young, hardened children on the street.

The first day I visited this community was a rainy Thanksgiving Day in 1985. The desperation of the people here was more extreme and of a different kind than that where any of us had worked before. Maria and I met and drove through Tijuana toward the east. It was late morning when we crested the hill overlooking the large valley. *Grupo Mexico* would later become home, hell and hope.

A political group with powerful leadership took over a large area encompassing numerous deep canyons. They quickly settled hundreds of very poor people on this land. The battle over the land kept tensions high for a number of years. Thousands of settlers became militant defenders of the invaded land. There were constant rumors of dissenting residents being beaten, murdered, and their homes set on fire with the non-conformists trapped inside.

As time went on, we developed a very good friendship and relationship with these leaders. They   provided us a better inside look at what was going on in the valley. The political leaders helped thousands of people who otherwise would not have been able to have a place to live. As the population swelled, so did the social unrest and problems. There was a lot more going on than met the eye. Drug trafficking, murder, crime and violence found an easy base of operation in these canyons. Since the city did not recognize the legality of the settlement, no city services, including police patrols, were provided. Every few months scrap metal dealers would come into the valley to haul out the stolen cars, stripped and burned, lining the rough dirt roads.

This and much more would come into focus over the next years. It all looked too innocent that Thanksgiving day. Blue tarps dotted the hillside. "Parachuters" they are called. Vacant land was quickly taken by families owning little more than a plastic tarp with which to cover themselves. We sloshed through the thick mud up a trail. It was cold.

Maria and I spotted an Indian woman; we approached her to inquire about the community.

As we walked, I couldn't help remembering, "Today is Thanksgiving." Not that it was significant in Tijuana. After all, the pilgrims didn't land in Tijuana, and there certainly wasn't anything I could see for which anyone could be thankful. This would be a most memorable and special day, like a breath of fresh air in the midst of choking smoke or a treasure found among ashes.

As we approached, the woman greeted us. We introduced ourselves. We stepped into her little eight by eight foot home. She stood barefoot in the mud with her three young children. Parts of the cardboard walls, soaked from the rain, had fallen to the ground. The water-soaked roof had fallen in as well. It was a bit awkward asking how they were, although she was kind and excited to have visitors.

"Where is your husband?" I asked. In broken Spanish, with a strong Indian accent, she told us that he had left them. She paused a moment then added, "But sometimes he comes back, drunk. And he beats us and hurts the children."

"What does he do to them?" we inquired. She quickly responded telling us in detail how he would grab the children's heads and while holding them over backwards he would mash chili peppers into their mouths.

We also asked where they slept and found that they were sleeping on a piece of cardboard in the small, now roofless, room. When we asked if they had any blankets, her reply was casual.

"No, we don't have a blanket, but we hug each other all night because it's been so cold." Maria and I shared glances; without a word spoken we both knew that we would be back.

"One more question before we go; do you have any food?"

"*Sí, gracias a Dios*--Yes, thanks to God," she answered. I was reminded again; today is Thanksgiving on the other side of the border. Thanksgiving--the giving of thanks.

She continued, "Yesterday we didn't have any food and the children were very hungry. But today, thanks to God, we have food." She had gotten up early that morning, and, taking an old sack, she had made her way through the rain and mud to the city. Behind a grocery store, in the trash bin, "thanks to God," as she said, she found some rotting corn. She trudged back through the valley and up the hill with her blessing.

Maria and I said good-bye, but before we could turn to leave, this poor woman reached out and said, "Please don't go; stay and eat with us." Needless to say, this was one of the most meaningful Thanksgivings I have ever experienced. We squatted there together and shared the boiled, rotten corn. They shared their only meal with us. I'll never forget her sincere smile as she stood with us, her children muddy and huddled together in the cold. No bed, no blanket, no roof, everything wet and cold.

"Yes, thanks to God, we have food today," she said.

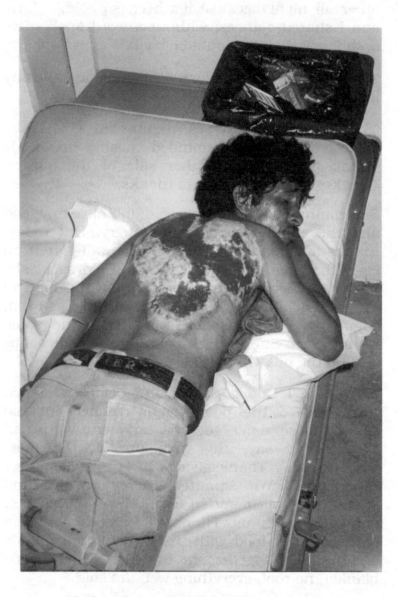

**Victim of a cruel prank. This man was
doused with fuel and set on fire.**

21
Constructive Help from Visiting Groups

In Grupo Mexico we had a fresh start. For years, groups other than our own wouldn't venture there. As the work progressed in this community, some of what had seemed to be slow progress in the beginning began to show positive results.

One aspect of our work was that of hosting visiting groups. Their work and help have been a great encouragement. Through such groups, more than 500 simple homes were constructed over a span of about seven years. Most of these groups demonstrated maturity, realistic ministry expectations and genuine love for the people. They worked hard, hand in hand with the folks from our Mexican church. The church had grown out of a number of ministries we had together with consistent teaching of God's Word. Pastors of the churches that came constantly encouraged me that this was a great training ground. Usually we would have some time to challenge and teach these visiting teams each night. Perhaps an impact was made, but at the time it didn't seem like much which would end up challenging anyone to further interest or involvement in this kind of ministry.

During one study with an American group, a local gang member who had attacked me months earlier came stumbling through the door begging for help. He was bleeding and had been stabbed and badly cut from chest to legs in a knife fight.

On another occasion, I was leading a visiting youth group up a canyon. Screams came echoing from one of the little make-shift houses, then out came two men fighting with knives. I don't think either of these events was a turning point to missions for our American visitors, to say the least. I took the loser to the hospital; we cleaned up all the blood out of the van and then had our study time with the group.

During one group visit, a man came running up the hill looking for me. He told me that a friend of ours, a man with many problems, was in the process of hanging himself. The American pastor group leader ran with me to the little house. The door was wired shut. We kicked in the door which knocked over a kerosene lamp, starting a fire. The man had fallen onto a bed with the wire noose still tightly twisted around his neck. We took the noose off my friend and carried him up to the church building; there the visiting high schoolers watched him during the night. When he finally gained consciousness, he reverted to being an unruly obnoxious drunk.

This church group is still, to this day, one of our supporting partners working with us!

Mostly our groups were from the U.S. and Canada, with a few exceptions of Mexican involvement from outside of Grupo Mexico. The reason more middle-class Mexican churches weren't involved in this community and others like it was not an economic issue, as many might believe. Working with a few of the more prominent pastors of Tijuana provided us a glimpse of an interesting approach toward reaching the lost.

I was asked by one Mexican pastor of a prominent Tijuana church why in the world would we want to work in an area with such a bad reputation, one so full of sin. Concerning the home building, he assumed that each family receiving a home would be forced to repent and become a Baptist. Although it was explained to him that, however great it would be that all would show interest in our motivation to serve, this was in no way connected to whom we would help. To him and a number of others, it was absurd helping homeless families who wouldn't "join the church." This interesting concept in "missions" eventually left my two Mexican partners and me so baffled as to what they perceived "serving Jesus" was all about, that we gave up pursuing efforts to work with these churches.

Our groups, however, were not interested in conning these poor people into raising their hands or bowing their heads or doing whatever one is supposed to do to become a proper "Christian." They simply came to give of themselves, sharing the simple love of Jesus through the testimony of their labor, working alongside their Mexican brothers and sisters, reaching out to the desperate. Perhaps it was this more sincere love which led many over the years to come to Christ. We have always maintained that short-term groups not be involved in any direct evangelism. We believe this is best done by those who really know the people. There is a whole lot behind this, which, when explained, makes perfect sense. Our groups understood these principles and therefore worked together very well with our local believers and led them to real and effective ministry.

Such is the story of Jose. A humble man, he lived with his wife and children huddled together in the stripped out shell of a leaky van. It was raining hard, a muddy, windy, cold day. I was with several Mexican brothers standing under a small plywood roof. We talked about the American group that was scheduled to come help build a house for Jose and his family. They were really hurting for any type of shelter. Jose wanted to take a bath and put on some clean clothes to look more presentable and look for a job. But with what water? With what clothes? They had no water containers, only a couple of small plastic bags holding all their worldly possessions. They were cold, wet and hungry. I had doubts that the U.S. group would come. Time passed.

Finally an excited call came, "Here they come; they are coming!" As the van slid from side to side in the mud, they made their way up the hill. The gloomy spirit was lifted. The rain had not stopped them. They had brought with them all the materials for building a small one room house. And, they were ready to go to work, rain or no rain.

Throughout the cold rainy afternoon, the group labored side-by-side with the men from our little church. In a few hours the house was up and Jose's family moved in.

We continued working with Jose's family.

Ultimately, they came to the Lord. Some people with similar stories, however, never responded. A few showed no gratitude whatsoever, while others were touched profoundly by the unconditional expressions of love. Some of those who became believers through our ministries eventually took the Bible teaching and returned to southern Mexico to share in other communities.

As for the visiting teams, they have blessed many by their ministry, and I am grateful for their partnership in the work. God has encouraged my heart through these churches, pastors, business professionals and youth groups who have participated as partners with us, supporting the growing vision. It has been through their sacrificial efforts that numerous aspects of the work were started. Through their partnership the ministries have grown and expanded, including teaching and discipling those with whom we work. Their facilitating this work allows us to offer educational and service opportunities to those who would otherwise not have them. The result of all this has been the growth of self-propagating, national-led ministries and missions from within the ranks of the poor.

We thank God for each of our ministry partners— some enabling the work through prayer, others through financial giving, others through their counsel and encouragement and others through providing personal accountability. When I consider all the lives profoundly and deeply touched through this work over all the years, I give thanks to God for each partner on the team that makes it all possible.

Overlooking Grupo Mexico valley

Work groups serving alongside Mexican partners

22

Life in the Barrio

As the ministry in Mexico grew larger, I grew smaller. I certainly hadn't planned to be a missionary. All I knew was that I wanted to serve others because of what God had done for me.

Life in this Mexican community was different than in past situations. Shortly after the little congregation started to grow there, we worked together to construct a simple 20' x 20' plywood meeting building ("church"). I hung my hammock there and left my work in San Diego. There was a tattered blanket which sufficed for a door. Mice and rats ran in and out through the gaps between the walls and the dirt floor. There were spiritually dark things which happened some nights. For the sake of "safe doctrine," I'll leave out the details. Then, there was the slow peeling back of the mask of social justice, exposing ugly reality. Senseless death and the poor getting shuffled aside in critical situations were all too common.

Time passed like sand running through an hourglass. The many experiences of those first days, weeks, months and years filled and molded my life. As some rough edges in my life were chipped away, others emerged. A collage began to form, a mixture of joy and pain, excitement and frustration, hope and despair.

A family knocked on the door early one morning and asked me to come help their child. The little girl was dead when I arrived. Late one night I awoke as someone fell against the outside wall.

After a moment, a voice repeated "You must learn to suffer, you must learn to suffer," I recognized the voice of a young man who lived a very dark spiritual life. He spoke in languages he had never learned.

Another night, a little girl called at the door. It was late. Her head was split open and she had dried blood matted in her hair, on her face and shirt.

"My Mom wants to know if you have some drinking water we can have," she said. I walked across the dusty dirt floor to pour some water, and as I did I asked what had happened to her.

She answered casually, "Oh, my dad came home tonight. He's drunk and beat me with a pipe."

Another day, a homeless, pregnant mother was found by one of our church members who took the woman into her humble home. In the course of helping this woman through her pregnancy, we accidentally uncovered a scheme in a public hospital which stole newborn babies. We took the story to the newspapers, which in turn went to the police to break the story. That was the wrong move. Police also were apparently involved. After the visit to the police, the newspaper reporter, in a nervous voice exhorted us to be quiet and forget we had seen anything. "Look, you got your baby back; just forget the whole thing," he told the woman.

A little girl's mother came to the church building late one night. She was crying and asked me to go see her little girl. We walked down the dark hill, across a ledge and up a steep bank to her home made of scrap materials. On the small dilapidated bed lay her daughter, seriously dehydrated, sick; her throat dry and swollen. The mother had taken her daughter to the hospital but had been turned away. We tried to get some liquids into her little body but she couldn't hold anything down. I did the best I could with her. We praised God that He spared her life. She was fortunate.

There was the young man brought to me by his family. They asked that I put him in our drug rehabilitation program. On top of having some drug problems, it was obvious that he was mentally disturbed. While the family talked, I listened, noticing how nervous this young man was. He had been in a fight recently. His opponent was unfortunate to have fallen. This young man lifted a large rock and smashed the other's head wide open, killing him. Since he was wanted by the Mexican police, I knew taking him into our program could potentially cause problems.

I asked him if it was his desire to enter our program and work on his drug problems. We talked a while before he got a terrified look in his eyes. He reached into his pants and pulled out a loaded pistol which he nervously pointed at me. This wasn't the first time I had looked down the wrong end of a gun; at least this time, if I were shot, I could take some consolation in being shot in the church I loved and served.

One night my van was having mechanical problems. It was almost midnight as I nursed the van out of the dark canyon. I pulled into a closed gas station to get water for the overheated engine; shortly after, a police car pulled in behind me. The officer looked around as he got out of his car, but I didn't think much about it. He asked what I was doing and then said I couldn't be at the gas station.

"I have to take you to the police station," he said. Despite my mechanical problems, he made me drive down an alley which I knew did, indeed, lead to a police station. Although I was thinking that he just wanted some money, I had second thoughts about his intentions when he stopped me a few hundred yards down the alley and took all my papers from me. I knew my van was in no shape to try anything, although I had a burning desire to throw it into reverse and try to launch this guy through his windshield. He directed me to drive further and then stopped me again and advised me that just ahead I was to turn in at an impound lot and then continue on in his police car. I started to wonder if I would be "disposed" of. The possibilities were getting worse. There were other police officials robbing a number of Mexicans when we arrived. Some of those crazy police nightmare stories that you hear are true. And, there are more you never hear. People just disappear. Life and business continue. One hand covers another.

There was a man who lived down the hill who had the habit of mixing drugs and alcohol. One night he came home completely cooked. He stormed through the door and pushed his young children across the room as he began to beat his wife with no mercy. The kids watched in horror as they always had. This time the little boy, about eleven years old, went outside to his father's car and, in aggravated frustration, broke out all the windows. He then grabbed his little six year old sister and ran up the hill. They arrived at my room, both obviously scared.

"Please hide us," he said. At the mother's request I kept the boy the next day and took him with me when I drove out to pick up some supplies. As we bounced over the rut-filled roads I asked, "If you could do anything in the world, anything at all, what would you do?"

He thought for a moment then looked into my eyes and asked, "Anything?"

"Yes, anything," I said.

He thought for a moment more and then, while looking straight ahead, he said, "First, I would tie up my dad. Then I would beat him until he couldn't take it anymore. And then, then I would shoot him in the head and then in the heart." So much for little boys' dreams of being astronauts and firemen.

Other events reminded me often that I needed to make the best of my time since my time seemed to be too frequently threatened. One night a drunk put a loaded gun to my head while rambling on about his hatred for Americans. Another night on the road, I came up behind one of the Mexican guys in my discipleship group. I had greeted him, but he did not respond, which was strange. I soon found out why when I approached and joined him looking down the wrong end of a gang member's gun. Then, there was the drunken tractor driver who tried cornering me against a dirt bank to crush me with the front loader of the tractor.

A close friend was shot one night in front of the church building. A couple of us arrived to find him lying face up in a puddle of blood. I had spent many days with him and his family. Although his wife became a believer, he was always too busy drinking and gambling to think much about what God might have for him. Not long after his murder, another young man was gunned down in almost the same spot. Sometimes folks seemed repulsed, other times relieved. Such was the time a group of the kids called me to come see the young man who had robbed and assaulted so many in the community. He was another to whom I and others had spoken many times. He had been stabbed numerous times, rolled up in a scrap of carpet and dumped on the side of the dirt road.

23

More Blessed to Give
Than to Receive

Although these and many other events made up part of the ministry landscape of our community, they could not and would not overshadow the purpose for which I was there. The word and life of Jesus Christ, His love, healing and treasure, discovered and multiplied. Boxed in the context of discipleship was the purpose of equipping others to teach, to give, to exercise their own faith and gifts, to be the giver and therefore the blessed. I believe our missions programs sometimes can be short on vision if our gratification is only in our own giving, serving, teaching and work. If we aren't also providing others with the opportunity to also give, serve, teach, work and to disciple others, we may actually not be doing so much at all.

Concerning the poor, it is most unfortunate that many foreign and national churches and ministries see them as nothing more than "ministry." The poor are rarely viewed as people also called of God and people whom God wants to use to do great things. They may be "ministry" today, yet in God's economy and purpose, be great "ministers" tomorrow--if we don't rob them of that opportunity. I have seen those who, many times are considered too poor to have much to offer; being greatly used by God to reach, teach and minister to those around them. Their sacrificial giving at times would shame some of the world's wealthiest churches.

If, as missionaries, we only give, we will rob those to whom we minister of a great blessing. Yes, it is more blessed to give than to receive. Along with giving ourselves, we must teach others to give. We may find ourselves humbled often by God's mighty work through those we teach. This is a principle I believe God ordained to edify His church through engaging us as disciplers and as disciples simultaneously.

Once, a family in our Grupo Mexico church sold all their simple possessions along with their humble home for a couple hundred dollars. They did so to have money to go back to southern Mexico to share the gospel. If that sounds extreme, that was only the beginning. A couple of days later they felt that God wanted them to give an offering to a missionary in South America where I was soon to go. They felt there was a bigger need there and besides, God could provide some other way for them. Little did they know, I could never find a missionary anywhere close to being as needy as they were. Here was a family with nothing but the little money from their house sale in hand, and they gave it all for a missionary they didn't know, in a land about which they knew nothing. They believed God would help them. That He did, providing for them through miracles some would find very hard to believe. I probably wouldn't have believed them myself, except that I saw them with my own eyes. To this family, it was no big deal. I again was humbled. Their faith made mine seem very small in comparison.

There are other such stories as well. One of the men came to me one day, and, as we talked, he expressed a desire to minister to a bunch of drunks living next to the railroad tracks; a place we called "El Campamento." Together we decided that a five month commitment would be appropriate in starting something there. In a short time this brother learned his first lessons in organizational skills.

This camp was an interesting place, a bunch of low-lying cardboard boxes arranged in a large circle. An old dried Christmas tree in the middle of the "village" and a human skull as its crowning ornament. Around the village, hanging on the brush were pieces of junk, miscellaneous trash and baby dolls tied up by their necks or feet. Garbage and mud surrounded the outside of the village. The men dug through trash dumpsters and brought home whatever looked more or less edible. When they finished eating, the scraps were simply tossed in the mud where the dogs, lots of dogs, would scavenge what might be left.

We walked through the trash and mud trying not to step in any deep spots. The dogs came out barking as we came near. One tipsy man crawled out of a box to see why the dogs were barking. We walked into the middle of the village and announced that we would like to talk with all the men. A few were relatively sober, a few tipsy, a few really drunk. We spoke with the men for a while and also told them that those interested in hearing God's Word were welcome at our church where we had added a Sunday night teaching time just for those curious in learning what God's message is all about. Apart from leading a weekly Bible study with them there, the Mexican brother with me would be happy to stop by for them each week and accompany them to our church.

Well, it wasn't but a few weeks later when he had his first "challenging" situation there. He got off the city bus, crossed the roadway and then walked down the trail to the camp. When he arrived he was told that one of the men was having trouble. A couple days earlier they said he had worked and had some money when he returned to the camp. The others had asked for it to buy more alcohol but he refused. So, after he had fallen asleep, one of the guys axed him in the head and took the money. They were concerned because he had not moved since, the ax still in his head.

Our new "missionary" started figuring how to handle this situation. First, he decided, he would get the drunks to the bus to the church service then he would return to see if the axed man was still alive.   After lining up all the drunks to run across the road when there was no traffic, he yelled, "Now." Everyone started running but a couple of the older men, who had had a few too many drinks, got disoriented half way across the road.

"Blump, blump." Those who had reached the other side turned to see what all the noise was. One of the guys had been run over by a car.

Our enthusiastic missionary was now pulling his hair out. He did a good job that night. After I finished the service we went to the Red Cross clinic where our friend was unconscious, but alive. The guy with the axe in his head also lived. All this eventually led to another ministry in the development of our drug and alcohol rehabilitation center! Our friend with the ax in his head became a believer there. Teaching others to give has its risks, but God can't work freely until we let things go. We must be responsible workers but not limit others' growth.

In most of our ministry we need to look way beyond simply ministering to others. We need to seek out how we can best help others reach their potential. This includes helping and encouraging them to do the same, discipling others to disciple others.

It is a blessing to receive, but it is more blessed to give. That's what our ministry is all about-- we strive to provide opportunities for folks to learn, grow, give and to disciple others to do the same.

El Campamento

Another public baptism

24

Eunie

It was a privilege to see God working dynamically in lives during those first years in Grupo Mexico. In those days, the local people were more dependent on each other and more open to ministry. As more destitute families filled the hillsides, God opened new avenues to share His love and His Word. A youth center was opened where a number of youth ministries served.

Various members from the local church helped in our medical clinic. Others worked with groups to build homes for homeless families, took prostitutes and other people living on the streets into their homes and sought out those poorer than themselves to whom to minister. A small drug rehabilitation program was developed. We prayed and walked the streets of the notorious "North Zone" of Tijuana and brought home with us those who we would literally pick up off the streets.

Our Sunday meetings always had some special, unplanned event. The men in the drug rehabilitation program would roll up their blankets as the people congregated to hear God's Word. At first our activities were not as diverse and we only had a 20' x 20' meeting room. Between 100 and 120 people would pack in each time of public teaching. Dogs and cats would also "attend" these meetings. It makes quite a stir, having a dog fight break out in the middle of service. From time to time, unruly drunks would come in. Once, a gang showed up and wanted to start a big fight. On numerous occasions, our services would be interrupted by nearby gun-fire. During one service, a young man was shot in the back and died in front of the church building.

The ministry saw many faces come and go through this transitional community. There we got to know many people from all over Mexico as well as Central and South America. Although some were illegally in Mexico, involved in illicit activities or in trouble and on the run, others were simple, struggling folks just needing some encouragement or help. God gave us opportunities to minister to all types.

Countless experiences and memories; some people saw God do miraculous works in their lives; others went their own way. Both sweet and bitter tears were tasted in Grupo Mexico.

One day, an intriguing young lady came to serve with a visiting team from the U.S. It was February 1988. This particular girl seemed to have the ability to get involved in the middle of some of our darker, uglier areas of ministry. She didn't mind the vomit, smells and sicknesses of our fresh arrivals in the rehabilitation center. She would quietly identify a need and simply go to work.

Over the following months and years, she would become an integral part of our Mexico team. Eunice is her name, although everyone calls her Eunie. She was born in Philadelphia of Taiwanese parents. Eunie grew up in a strong Christian home. Her father started many Bible study groups and founded the Evangelical Formosan Church which has developed into a denomination of more than fifty churches in six countries. Her home as a youngster was full of gratitude and appreciation. Eunie tells a story of growing up with little of what others might call basic necessities of life. It was much later in life that it dawned on her how little they lived on. Their family poured everything they were and everything they had into the churches her dad was serving. Eunie remembers how her parents were always content with what they had, thankful and sincerely grateful for the simple things.

Prior to Eunie's first trips to Mexico, she was very involved in her church's ministries to the homeless, the elderly, the junior high group, those in convalescent homes and the poor in Los Angeles. Even before her trip to Mexico, a year prior she had dedicated her life to serving God on some mission field.

I was impressed with her dedication, hard work and sacrificial spirit. She never had a harsh word, and I never heard her complain. We developed a good working relationship. Since I wasn't interested in marriage and made that fact known, we had a good friendship centered around the ministries we shared.

For several years I tried to set her up with friends I felt would make a good partner for her. She didn't have time for dating though. She had a full-time job, helped at her church and for a number of years led a Friday night youth group in Los Angeles. After the Friday night youth meetings, she would drive two hours to arrive in our dark barrio south of the border.

On Saturday and Sunday mornings at 6:00 a.m., I taught a chronological Bible study. We avoided more interruptions from drunks at that hour. After the Saturday morning study, Eunie would serve around the community on her own and then clean and bring order to our disorganization in the rehabilitation center in the evenings. Sunday mornings after the 6:00 a.m. study, she would drive the two hours back north to teach a Sunday school class in her own church. Her home church eventually commissioned her as their church's first missionary.

God would change my heart and position and give me a love never experienced before in my life. The first considerations I gave to marriage came during a year I spent in the Amazon in 1992-1993. It took a while to settle everything, but when I was sure this was God's next step for me, I waited for Eunie's next birthday to propose to her--October 1996. What a proposal!

I was not under any delusion. I felt my proposal had some scary implications for her. For me, I would marry an angel; she would marry something much less! We were married August 30, 1997. Writing this page, it's already been more than five years of a wonderful marriage. She is still an angel, and I am afraid that I am still not much more than a redeemed devil!

I couldn't have asked for a better partner. Eunie gives herself 100% to everything she does: cutting lumber with a chainsaw in South America, counseling messed up young girls on the street, working with the women in the communities where we minister, cooking for our staff and students during our training courses in different parts of Latin America. In addition, preparing teaching materials in Indian dialects, putting together our Spanish teaching materials to typing and laying out this book you hold-- Eunie gives her all! I am blessed in every way to be married to her. We are very blessed to serve together, working out the vision we share with those who partner with us.

Shortly after getting married, Eunie joined me on a short trip to Venezuela. In addition to having the opportunity for her to get to know numerous old friends of mine there, I took her to a village of the Indians with whom I have spent much time. Eunie has a good humored spirit but was not enthused by my joking one day.

Several Indian ladies walked by the missionaries' house heading to a jungle stream to search for crabs. I started complaining to them. The ladies were a little upset at all I said, which was exactly what I had intended!

"What are you saying to them?" Eunie asked.

"I'm telling them how angry I am that they are going crabbing. Here we are so hungry, that you really know how to crab and that you want to go with them. They said tomorrow you can go with them, but then I heard one of them say, 'That foreigner can't really know how to crab.' "

I yelled back, "My wife certainly knows how to crab. Tomorrow, you will just see that she really knows."

Eunie looked forward to going with the ladies until I gave her a few words of caution the following morning. "Be careful and watch out for snakes. There are also electric eels under the rocks. Sometimes scorpions and stinging ants are in the foliage around the edge of the streams."

My words of caution seemed to reduce Eunie's enthusiasm for the big crab hunt. Nevertheless, she was off with the ladies. The day started with canoeing up the river, then taking a trail a short distance to the stream. On the way, one girl was chased down the trail by a snake which repeatedly lunged at her as it chased her.

Arriving at the stream the ladies dove in up to their shoulders, plunging their arms into the dark nooks and crannies. Eunie, still thinking about the snake and the electric eels, poked a little here and there with a stick, but didn't crab with the enthusiasm the Indian women had expected. The commentaries were endless, "Look at her; she certainly doesn't know how to crab. She doesn't know. The foreigner doesn't know."

I felt bad that I had built up Eunie's crabbing ability so much in the eyes of the Indian women. Each of the Indian women had caught at least one crab. The only remedy seemed to simply defend her ability, even in the light that she had not captured even one crab. That was the Indian thing to do. These fresh water crabs are all about hand size.

It was our delight to later send, through a missionary friend, a photo for these same Indian women. Eunie had her photo taken in a big U.S. fish market holding up some giant ocean crabs. You can imagine their comments upon seeing that photo. "They weren't lying. Look, she really does know how to crab!"

**My wife isn't afraid of snakes and eels.
She really knows how to crab!**

Eunie visits villages, 1998

25

Living in the Dog House

Through the love, partnership and generous help of our ministry partners, principally in the USA and Canada, Eunie and I have been undeservingly blessed to have a home in our home country.

When Eunie and I began discussing marriage, we had no idea how we would afford a home. My brother-in-law found a piece of relatively inexpensive property just north of San Diego. Even though there was a house on the property, it was for sale as "land value only." The property was located between several flower growing "green houses" on a dirt road.

The old house was literally falling down. A separate garage and attached dog kennel were in no better shape. Surrounding the house were countless truckloads of junk, trash, drug needles and paraphernalia from the druggies who had occupied the vacant house. After praying, we decided to purchase the property together with my sister, Sherry, and her husband, Steve. When my parents went to see the property, my mom broke down crying.

We took our savings together with generous help from our parents and a few friends and went to work. Together with Steve and Sherry, we worked many long nights and days fixing up the old house into which they moved.

Next, Eunie and I started gutting the dog kennel to turn it into an apartment for us. I've never liked dogs, so it's a bit ironic that we ended up, literally, in the dog house! The old dog kennel conversion worked out great, and we are grateful for God's provision of what turned out to be a very nice home.

After getting married, we had the blessing of having "a home away from home"--a place in San Diego as well as our room in Mexico. Since that time, the bumpy dirt road has been paved, the wild rabbits and coyotes have been replaced by new neighbors, the "greenhouses," all torn down now, have been replaced by very expensive custom homes.

Even before marrying, Eunie and I made some decisions about our work which we knew very well would leave us with virtually no time off from our little world of ministry for a number of years. So, all the more, it has been a giant blessing having a home in San Diego, since part of our work has us north of the border as well as south.

Rick and Eunie

26

Discipleship and a New Church

Although the goal is to serve, it goes a bit further than that. God has surrounded us with supportive partners who share a common conviction—that outreach to the poor is not good outreach if not coupled with discipleship, teaching and opportunity. Even though this may present a difficult challenge because of the precepts which cause and fuel poverty, it must be done if these are to become future teachers, disciplers and leaders effectively reaching others.

This is no small task in any society. Look at the challenges Jesus faced with his disciples! Look at the challenges He faces in discipling us! The core of a life being transformed sits in a shift of values and world view. The more we embrace God's values and a Biblical world view, the more we are transformed.

I guess it's most always easier to exclusively "minister to" others rather than to "serve with" others, providing appropriate discipleship, training and equipping to see others do the same. Perhaps that partially explains why so many of our modern churches have more of a "classroom" or "platform" format centered heavily around meetings rather than a "modeling" format in which leaders teach by doing as opposed to lecturing. It takes a lot of time. It comes many times, with hurts, disappointments and set backs. Through it all, we can sincerely say it has been a blessing to work with so many great people. Some of these great folks which were our "ministry" of yesterday are now responsible "ministers" today.

In early 1994, we organized a team of student-workers from the Grupo Mexico church to work with us in a new settlement east of Tijuana. I returned from a year working back in the Amazon. Returning to Mexico, working with Juan, we organized this student-worker outreach. It started with a lot of prayer. Some of the team members came out on Saturdays or Sundays to learn and work. A few moved to the new settlement.

As far as teaching, they were very nervous. Our work had decisively changed gears here. We would teach others to teach. The goal of the team would be to raise a new church in which all the leaders of the church would eventually be from that new group of believers. I wouldn't be the pastor. The student-workers, although learning and leading the new church, wouldn't be the pastors. We would work, teach and disciple with the objective of seeing men and women reached, taught, equipped and raised up to lead their new church and to lead new outreach.

Although there were plenty of ups and downs and challenges over the first six or seven years, God used the faithful members of the team in a powerful way to do just that. They faced doubt and even criticism along the way. There were some, even a few pastors, who strongly communicated that the team could never learn to teach and lead effectively. The team--although many times nervously so--kept their eyes on God, their confidence in His Word, His commission, His ability and, as always, He is faithful.

Eight years later, a small congregation in Terrazas del Valle stands on its own. The church is being led by its own, men who are serving and pastoring together, leaders doing a good job, working together, a team.

Although the church is small, in a very poor settlement, with extremely limited resources, it has been greatly blessed. This congregation has sent out its own missionary, actually three, and is providing their support--through incredible sacrifice. In cooperation with the Grupo Mexico church, they sent out other families, also supporting them spiritually, materially and economically as they have reached out to a mountain village even poorer than their own settlements.

The meetings at the small church vary in length. During these last years, the "time to give thanks" part of the service has typically lasted between 30 minutes to well over an hour. We will no doubt never be awarded any prize for great singing but God knows it's from the heart. Sometimes some of the best teaching comes from the "time to give thanks" when thanksgiving becomes exhorting from the Word.

The offering time isn't a plate that is passed around. In the privacy of the back corner of the room is a small wood box. As part of the worship, families or individuals get up at random, walk to the corner, pray, give thanks and give what God has put on their heart. What is usually on their hearts to give is a whole lot more than most would imagine.

The teaching or instruction time is practical, for the equipping of the congregation, for the ministry and the building up of the church.

The small but serious group has really inspired Eunie and me. Their ministry has stood in great contrast to the image left engraved in my mind by the pastor of one of Tijuana's oldest Christian churches, a church boasting some of the city's elite. Shaking his head, he assured me some twelve years ago that work in these communities is a waste of time. Ministry in settlements where crime, violence and lawlessness reign would be fruitless. God has done great things in lives here which have given testimony to who He is.

These following words of testimony and exhortation come from a recent "thanksgiving" time during a Sunday meeting.

The man who spoke is not yet a Christian. He came to a Sunday meeting out of curiosity about what he had seen happen in the life of his friend. "I also want to give thanks to God. I am seeing that God is great and powerful. I am here because I've seen how God has changed my good friend. I know how he used to live; drugs and evil ruled his life. Since my good friend here heard these studies of God's word and believed in Him, his life has been totally changed. I want you all to pray for me, because I want to hear these words of God so that I can hear and understand and believe like my good friend has. I give thanks to God although I don't yet know Him, but I see how great He is."

27

A Poor Church Sends
Its First Missionaries

In the Grupo Mexico and Terrazas del Valle churches, God continues to work. In Terrazas del Valle, our original, small discipleship group has multiplied. It's not a big group today either, but it has spread out while demonstrating strong roots.

Jose, one of the student-workers from the Grupo Mexico community, became more involved in the chronological Bible teaching outreach which had developed over the years. Although he had heard the Bible taught as a single story while in Grupo Mexico, it became more powerful in his life as he began to share it with others in Terrazas del Valle.

In 1995, we began developing more of these teaching resources in Spanish. Although originally intended for just our small group, they started to find enthusiastic acceptance in other Latin American ministries. Jose began taking the materials, audio teaching tapes, illustrations and later a teaching manual Eunie and I put together, to other Mexican churches. Wonderful things have happened in many of these churches and Jose has been sharing this blessing, multiplying workers, teachers and help in Mexican churches ever since.

Not only has this phase of the work grown in Mexico, but has encouraged and helped churches, schools, ministries and training centers throughout the Spanish speaking world:

Argentina, Bolivia, Colombia, Cuba, Panama, Paraguay, Spain and Venezuela. We continue to provide a training course at the invitation of groups in these countries. In Mexico, we work with Jose and others in seeing this opportunity provided to a growing number of churches and ministries. God has recently expanded this outreach together with challenging Mexican churches in world missions through the hard work of Octavio Jimenez. Octavio, a chemical engineer, joined our Mexican board of directors, overseeing our sister mission in Mexico. He is also a missions promoter and has left his chemical profession to serve in this ministry full-time.

We had only been in Terrazas a few years when I took Jose to see with his own eyes the things I had shared with him and the church many times, that of true cross-cultural mission work. I took him to visit a veteran missionary friend in the Sierra Madre Mountains working with the Tarahumara Indians. Jose's life was profoundly impacted when visiting that missionary and Mexican Indians with whom he could not communicate in Spanish; they knew only their tribal language. The experience poured over into Jose's visits with other churches. He challenged them to get involved in serious mission efforts.

Shortly after returning to Terrazas del Valle, Jose shared the things he had seen, heard and learned deep in the Sierra Madre mountains. No one would have ever imagined that on that day, three children would take the missionary challenge deep to heart. Three of our early-on group members were these three youngsters. Their mother had recently died and the father was often gone from the home on illicit trafficking runs into the USA.

These three kids were involved in every outreach the church group offered. They became very strong believers over the years. No one knew that Jose's testimony had impacted them so deeply. However, on that day, these three kids started praying in their small house and continued praying.

Life became harder. Their father disappeared for a long time and they found out much later that he had been caught and imprisoned in California. An older brother stepped in to help the three, but shortly after he got into a fight with a guy and killed him. So the older brother was put in a Tijuana prison. Amelia, the oldest, had to work a full-time job, try to finish her elementary education and, at the same time, care for her younger sister and the youngest—little Antonio.

One day Amelia asked if the three could talk to all the men of the church. They explained that after spending much time in prayer, they had come to the conclusion that Amelia should go be a missionary to a group of Indians like they had heard of in Jose's testimony and had seen in my videos of other places.

Many things happened over the following months. The men started talking together about sending Amelia, but were soberly quiet when they discovered how much money it would cost to send her to the New Tribes Mission missionary training. Never did they blink. They were sure this was the right thing, even if it would cost the families of the church food from their tables.

Another question was what would happen to the younger ones. After Amelia was accepted for the four year training course, Eunie and I began to really consider what might happen to the children. One day I got together with nine year old Antonio to ask him if he really understood what Amelia would be leaving to do. He looked up and gave a clear and precise answer, "She will go far away where she will learn the Bible real good so that she can go share it with the Indians."

"You know this is a school for big people, Antonio, and you won't be able to go," I said.

Antonio looked up into my eyes and confidently said, "I already know that."

I asked him a number of other similar questions to which each time he looked up at me and made it known that he knew these things and had already thought about them.

I had been skirting the possibility of his having the misfortune of perhaps being separated from his other sister and taken away to an orphanage. When I raised the question, Antonio answered the same way saying, "And I know that too."

In asking what he thought about the possibility of being separated from his sisters and perhaps maybe never seeing them again, he responded,

"What I think is that maybe that's what I can do so that the Indians can also hear God's Word."

Miracles. Some small, some large. God made it possible for all three to go together. The impossibility of sending and supporting one was suddenly multiplied to three. Fewer than fifteen families in the church would gather around these three, lay their hands on them, pray for them and send them off to a far-away training school. It would not be easy, but God would greatly bless the sacrifices, creative efforts and commitment of the small church.

With great conviction they sent out their first representatives towards the mission field. To not fall captive to dependency or compromising the conviction they took so seriously, they graciously turned down an offer from a USA church which offered to help them support their missionary. They firmly decided that they would "look up" rather than "look north" for God's provision. It is indeed more blessed to give than to receive. Four years passed. The little church fully and completely supported those they had sent out. Amelia graduated and now works as a missionary.

Our community multi-purpose "ministry vehicle"

50 gallon drum baptisms

28

Prayers, Priorities and Pesos

During those years, one of the men in my discipleship group greatly impressed me early one morning. We had finished praying with the others and he asked to talk to me privately. We walked out behind the outhouse. He told me he had received a small unexpected bonus at the factory where he worked. He went on to say that he and his wife had made a list of their priorities for using this money.

Before he could finish his sentence, I envisioned what some of those priorities might be. Some roofing paper to patch the leaking roof, some cement to plaster the walls of scrap wood of his house where the wind, dust and dirt blew through, or a little concrete on part of the house's dirt floor. My racing thoughts were interrupted when he put a roll of peso bills in my hand and said, "My wife and I decided together what the priority is. This money should go to help the group of Indians working with the missionary to put the Bible into their Indian language."

There have been other such offerings. The result of this vision has been God's blessing in, on and through the church. And the result of the blessings has been further giving. This has all been born out of prayer. Members of the church join together to pray; they pray for the sick and hurting, for those who are being taught, those who are teaching and for the different missionaries they have. One group meets together every week and prays for their missionaries. Others pray at home. One individual gets up to pray at 3:00 a.m. and has an extensive list over which he prays.

Here it is now, years later. Most of the original believers are also "ministers," each involved in some way, teaching in the community, serving, ministering, helping others more needy than themselves and reaching out beyond their own community. The small church has sacrificed to send out others, and they continue to be greatly blessed.

Although the church is small and money poor, they have a great stake in God's work. The stories are many of the help, the offerings, the ministry and the encouragement they have sent out near and far.

One of the church leaders took a night job. It had a number of benefits in his way of seeing things. He could work all night, take a couple hours to rest in the morning and evening and have all day to serve those in the community and church.

God sent Eunie and me to work in this community, to equip the student-workers who gave of themselves to serve there, to see a new church raised up. We have been blessed beyond measure by our time with each individual in both

Grupo Mexico and Terrazas del Valle and have certainly learned as much as we have ever taught.

Eunie and I look forward to hearing the Lord's words to these folks, "Well done, good and faithful servants; enter into the joy of your Master." Our joy will be complete in seeing them and others we have come to know through the years in God's presence. This will, no doubt, be a wonderful part of eternity for all those who are the real heroes, those who have faithfully partnered with us over many years making all these things possible!

**Picking up sick drug addicts in
La Zona Norte--Tijuana**

**Grupo Mexico residents march to the prison
to seek the release of their leader**

Rick with Grupo Mexico leaders, late 1980's

29

Tomorrow May Not Be

All of us, as partners in what God is doing to reach the world today, want to make a significant impact. Sometimes we might miss the greatest opportunities if we think of "significant" in terms of big—big programs, big numbers or lots of people rather than the significance and importance of one life, each single life. Your life is important and the God of the universe values *you*. You are a significant individual and so are those around you.

Although Jesus did great things before large crowds, he usually walked away when the people became most impressed. He didn't want followers who were impressed. He wanted followers who believed, really believed. That is what He taught throughout his entire ministry. Therefore we need to view ministry in this same light. Although we want to be part of the big and exciting things, we need to be focused on individuals, the significance of each one we have opportunity to serve.

Too many times we may find ourselves tempted to "do missions" much like one tries to win it big at the horse races. We look at the odds and try to pick the "winner projects." Many of the missionaries we know purposely didn't choose winning projects.

They chose the ones which were the "losers" to give them opportunity. That's what our little ministry has endeavored to do; to hold high that which in the normal economy of things would not be.

We must not view ourselves too positively, for we all can fail; nor too poorly, for God's mercy can lift us up. No one is a lost cause completely until there are no more opportunities. Some with whom we work may be very close to experiencing a new life, God's grace and peace. Life's road is a mix of small miracles and those which could have been. The keys may be in the door, but the door not opened. We will always wonder if we did enough while at the time exhausted from doing all we could.

There's the family who so graciously took me in, fed me and helped me when I first moved into the Grupo community after leaving my construction work. For years I shared with the man of that home. We had a good friendship. In his own way he was respectful and considerate of our Christian views, even when many Sunday mornings he would stand across the road, drunk and mock our church meetings. With a liquor bottle raised in his hand, he would attempt to sing our songs. Our singing was generally so poor that his drunken attempt was, at times, as good as that of the congregation. It was more humiliating than mocking! During his more sober moments, we had some good talks. "Some day I may believe these things you are sharing with me," he would say. "Yes, some day, but not now."

One night, Eunie and I and a couple of others from the church went up the rough dirt road. We found my friend there in the middle of the road. His keys were in the door, but the door was not opened. Before he could get into his house, he had been attacked and beaten, dragged into the middle of the dirt road and stabbed to death. He died in a puddle of blood in the same spot where we had so often talked. As I turned my flashlight into his open but lifeless eyes, I remembered his words, "Some day. Yes, some day...."

In a similar situation, there was another young man in the community with whom I had talked many times. Although he had many opportunities, he never seemed to have time to think much about the implications of his life, his activities or the greater things of life he could experience from God's Word. I saw him on the day his opportunities ceased to be. When I saw him that day, he was dead. His face was swollen, his body picked full of stab wounds. His younger brother followed his criminal footsteps and was recompensed being burned alive when his little house was set on fire.

Let's look again at the important things of life. As far as making a significant impact, we would do well to realize that our time is limited. It is limited in many ways. Limited time also means limited opportunities, only available as long as there is life. And life itself is all too fragile.

One day we found a young man on the edge of a path on his back, dead. Whoever left him there didn't even bother stealing his watch. Although I noticed that his watch kept perfect time, he had lost his opportunity to utilize it. Oh how we need to see today as a day of opportunity, the day of salvation and all the more our day of opportunity to reach out to those around us. Tomorrow may not be.

Other experiences come to mind: lessons, thoughts, considerations and challenges.

Spending the night with a young Indian boy in the Amazon; he was unconscious, convulsing, worms pouring out of his nose and mouth. Malaria almost killed him that night. He finally got better and returned to his village, only to be re-infected and die a short time later.

During fighting between two Indian groups, things got fairly bad. Word was radioed out and the Venezuela National Guard was flown in. After the planes left, things got worse. I was named to take the captives and the National Guardsmen down river by night. The Indian who accompanied me and I were almost killed in an accident on the river. The guards were scared and overreacted. We got everything back together and continued down river in the dark. When we came close to an enemy village, I wanted to pass and keep going through the night. The captain, however, ordered me to pull up to the bank. They went into the village shooting and then laid us all out under the watch of a nervous machine gun totting guard all night. The next two days with these guys is another story. Opportunities come in the strangest packages.

There's the death of a very dear missionary friend. That same week, five Indians also died of malaria. A few years later another close friend, a missionary in Colombia, was taken hostage and killed. These servants and a few other friends also died as a consequence of their service; some living out their service, others dying in the middle of it. Great men and women, humble servants, dedicated in life, steadfast in death.

Then there are the brothers and sisters in the Grupo Mexico and Terrazas del Valle churches in Tijuana. A good number have excelled in love, faith and mercy. Their lives stand out as beacons of light and example. Their sacrifices, service and giving have served as an inspiration to hundreds who have heard of their testimony. Some, from their daily bread, have joyfully sacrificed so that others might have the opportunity of hearing God's Word. Although the numbers fluctuate, as this is being written, almost 100% of the church families and/or individuals are involved in teaching other families in surrounding communities or serving in missionary outreach! They take opportunity to serve today; tomorrow may not be. Each individual is significant in God's eyes.

One of the many rivers to cross

Heading to a village hard hit by malaria epidemic

30

Poison

Although a number of sad situations have crossed our path as a couple, there is one in particular which will always stand out to us.

His gang name was "Veneno," venom or poison in English. He was a rough and mean young man who headed up the local gang in the community in which we serve. Although we would often walk by their hangout as we went out to visit different families together, rarely would the gang ever really talk a lot to us, although we always spoke to them.

This changed one summer day. Veneno hung himself on the basketball court down the road. He was cut down and lived. Less than two weeks later, a truck slowly came down the road. Veneno was on the corner of the road when the truck drove up. From out of the back of the truck some young men began shooting. Veneno started to run, but a bullet struck him in the back and he fell to the ground. His pursuers turned him over and beat his face and head with the butts of their rifles. They left him for dead. He did not die, but was left paralyzed. He led his gang from the restraints of a wheel chair.

We went and visited Veneno a few times before we were to lead a team from the church on a missions trip. Returning from the trip, we found Veneno in his small dirt floor room restricted to his bed. Upon entering the small room, there was a rancid smell of rotting meat. I spoke with him about his back and the bullet still lodged in his spine. Veneno--Steven being his real name--said to me, "There is something worrying me more than my back." He pulled his blanket down as far as he physically could. I helped pull it down to his feet. His legs and hind side were rotting, complicated by his having no control of his bowels. Excrement contaminated his rotting wounds.

The next day Jose, one of our team partners, took Steven to a Christian hospital where he was shamefully treated. After Jose's coaxing and payment, they cleaned out the rotted flesh. Jose returned him to his bed, now with his leg bones exposed.

I took Eunie with me to change his bandages. Her careful and compassionate touch combined with a caring smile detracting from the rancid smell which would even gag Steven when the old bandages were removed. Steven slowly got worse. Jose took him to the general hospital and argued with doctors who did not want to admit him. Jose embarrassed them to the point that one doctor admitted Steven. Steven later left the hospital with a colostomy which greatly helped us in keeping his wounds from being so badly contaminated.

I was deeply touched by Jose and his wife's efforts, as well as a number of others from the church who helped in different ways under very unpleasant conditions. They aided us in changing Steven's bandages, but he was slowly dying.

The Christian hospital offered no further help, although one of their doctors came on his own time to visit Steven numerous times over the months. Steven's condition and rotting became so severe that his leg bones often became detached and had to be wrapped back in place.

Every Friday, Eunie would take the blankets all soaked in bodily fluids and spend hours washing, disinfecting and folding them for the next week. There were other tasks she took on that were very unpleasant, although her disposition didn't reveal it.

Many stories have a good ending. Steven's didn't. Although Steven became a believer and strongly embraced God's forgiveness, he never had the opportunity to return and give thanks as the leprous man did in Luke 17. We prayed together often during his final months. I learned from Steven what the depth of repentance can be. Eunie continued to wash the blankets; I dressed his wounds. During the week, others from the church would also visit and help.

The men from the church and I had to go on a trip. We had the opportunity to put Steven in our rehabilitation center where Juan was then director. The men there embraced him as an opportunity to serve and help. The men encouraged him all day long, fed him; one man changed his bandages and watched over him. Steven was so happy in the rehabilitation center.

He even started to gain some weight and had a better outlook on life. But an American missionary who, at that time, was financing the rehabilitation program, didn't want Steven there. He was an "unproductive member."

I'll never forget the day Juan was forced to call me and advise me that we had to take Steven out of the center. It is such a sad story I can't tell it all. It was a cool night when two Mexican friends and I drove up the hill to take Steven home to die. When Steven realized why I had come, he began to cry. I left the room to ask Juan if there was any way to work it out for him to stay. Juan wanted to, but had his hand forced. He didn't have a choice.

It was totally silent as I changed his bandages and wrapped everything together as best I could. I'm crying now just thinking about it. As I pushed his wheelchair out the door, all the men in the rehabilitation center lined up on both sides of the narrow path. No one spoke a word; Steven stared straight ahead.

We put Steven in the back of the van. I cradled the wheelchair as we went down the rough road. Steven began screaming in pain from the bullet still lodged in his back. I tried to cushion the bumps the best I could and prayed with my friend as we slowly went down the road. It took a little more than an hour to arrive back home, although it seemed longer. Before we could get back to our settlement, his leg bone had fallen out and his tail bone was protruding.

Upon arrival, we wrapped him up in one piece the best we could and put him in his room. The men of the church had taken sacrificially from their limited funds and time to pour a nice cement floor, making Steven's room cleaner and more attractive. Eunie and I continued to visit him during his final weeks. Eunie continued to do some horrendous tasks.

Steven was yellowing; his kidneys were failing; he was dying. We did all that we could. Although Steven became a believer, he never had the opportunity to walk in Christ here.

The last day he was alive, we talked a good while. I was feeling resentful towards the Christian hospital, the American who had him leave the rehabilitation center and the lack of help from the general hospital. At the same time I was proud of, grateful for and impressed with the servanthood of all those in the church who sacrificially helped, for Eunie's work and for Jose, but our friend was now close to his end. As we talked, I leaned over and said, "Steven, you are going to die. Your confidence in Jesus will soon have you with Him. Steven, although you can't walk now, you will soon. When I meet with you again, we will take a very long walk together." He gave me his affirmation and then asked me to pull him up higher in his bed. A few hours later, he went blind and died a terrible death.

To the last day, Eunie made special meals for Steven, cleaned his soaked blankets and shared mercy and grace. Together with Jose and the church members who became the friends of a violent gang leader, abandoned by his own, we look forward to doing with him in heaven what couldn't be done here--walk, fellowship and rejoice in God's grace together with a young man named Veneno.

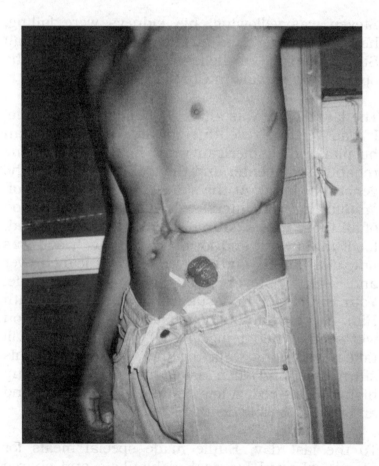

Attacked by the local gang, a young man had his stomach cut open

31

Los Diabólicos

Camping isn't something I would choose as a hobby. It's probably because so much of my missionary life seems to have been in some ways a very long camping trip. To the youth with whom we work, the word "camp" seems to always bring a lot of excitement. For some of our kids, it's just the thrill of getting out of the barrio, to others it's a big adventure and for some of the poorer kids, it's like going to a five-star hotel! I guess a lot of people see camping as "roughing it," but to some of these kids it's no such thing. Your very own place to sleep, a bath and three meals a day! What else could one want?

For many years we participated in a yearly camp sponsored by Von and his ministry. A few years ago I considered ending this part of our program with these little angels!

I drove the big bus up the steep dirt road. Although it was still quite early, most of the kids were out waiting in front of the simple church building, the first of three stops. We had invited a number of youth from the local gang "the Diabólicos." We knew this camp would be rough. The expectations were re-explained to the kids, especially the gang kids. Three main things we asked of them. No smoking on the bus, no weapons or fighting and no drug use at camp. We didn't want to scare them away with a big list of rules. Just complying with these three would be challenge enough!

I kept an eye on my gang kids who, of course, sat in the very back of the bus. I wouldn't get staff help until the next stop. Soon their heads were down below the bus seats and the strong odor of paint thinner filled the bus.

The purpose of this particular camp was to give about sixty rough teens a unique opportunity to hear God's Word, attend a camp and see that they really are loved. Accomplishing this goal would not be easy. The road trip was only a few hours, although it seemed much longer. I drove the bus. Two other vans went also.

Before we arrived at camp, a good percentage of the youth were fairly cooked from doing drugs, sniffing glue and paint thinner. One of the larger staff members found himself immediately surrounded by ready to fight gang members when he intervened to stop the beating of another boy. One boy had his teeth knocked out by one of his fellow campers. This was just the beginning of day one of a three-day camp! How nice it would have been to have hosted a bunch of Christian Girl Scouts instead of these teen boys. The staff did a great job against all odds.

Although we had a number of competitive games which they all loved, there were so many other activities it's hard to know where first prize should have been awarded. The drugs, fights, stealing, breathing thinner and glue, alcohol and graffiti among our "organized" activities!

On day two we took the best behaved youth deep sea fishing. Thirty-four kids piled onto the bus. About a half hour before getting to the dock, I stopped to give each kid a seasick pill. I took two, not wanting to take any chances.

Arriving at the dock, our thirty-four fishermen jammed onto the fishing boat. What a wonderful wholesome experience for these youth. Their first time on the high seas, a boat adventure, fishing! As the boat made its way out into the ocean and through the large waves, I started not feeling so well. I went down below to some bunks in the bottom of the boat to lie down. We kept going, and going, and going.

After a while I started wondering how far away from shore we were. We had been motoring out for a good while. Finally the engines cut back and it seemed to me we were in calmer water. I got out of the bunk and climbed back up to the deck. I couldn't believe my eyes; we were back in the harbor! For the most part the kids were all quietly standing around the edge of the boat. The seasick medication had worked for some of them but not for others who had become sick while heading out through the waves.

Street survival skills had instinctively kicked in for a couple of these youth. They simply took the filet knife out of the bait tank and climbed pirate style up to the captain. Putting the knife to his throat, they told him to turn the boat around and head back. With a simple flash of the knife against the captain's throat, the fishing trip was over. Nobody seemed too upset by the experience nor was there any apparent disappointment that we had gone on a fishing trip but had not once put a single hook in the water!

Everyone just seemed happy to be back on dry land. Back at camp the other kids were expecting the big catch for the planned fish fry. To avoid a riot, we bought a big fresh tuna from the fish market which the gang proudly presented upon arriving back at camp. No one dared to reveal where it had actually come from.

Although I'm not much for "camping" like this, it was a profitable time. We earned an open door to be able to work with these kids. A few of them have listened well. The darkness and oppression they live in daily in the rough barrios is the challenge of a lifetime of ministry.

Our church bus

32

You Need To Have Faith

God works on behalf of those who know they can't. Exodus 3-4 is a perfect example of this. Here we encounter Moses finding all kinds of excuses for not being the man for the job God gave him of freeing the Israelites from their slavery. Moses says, "Who am I to go? I don't have the words. They won't believe me. I'm not a good speaker." You can almost hear a whisper through the text, "It's not who you are, Moses; it's who I am. You don't have the words; I do. They won't believe you, but they will believe Me. You are a terrible speaker, but I will be with you. That's why I'm sending you. You know you can't do it. I will be with you."

A South American missionary I first met in the mid-1980's in Colombia had to leave the primitive Indian group he and his family were serving in Venezuela. Since they were unable to return to their remote tribe, they focused on training other Latins for cross-cultural missions. God has not only allowed them many opportunities to train others, but to also reach out in unique ways no others have.

In partnering with this ministry, we saw a need a couple of years ago that we knew would be a challenge to meet. Part of the vision was to open a training center in a remote wooded area similar to where many missionary candidates might work. A tractor, a truck, generators, tools, river transportation and educational materials would be needed. These things would be very expensive and cost more in Venezuela than what any of us could possibly afford. Another complication was the unavailability in Venezuela of some of the things needed. We all prayed together. Together with this missionary couple, Eunie and I made a trip out to the remote training grounds and prayed about all the impossible obstacles.

Over the next year, 2000, many little miracles came together. No fundraisers, no soliciting, God brought His people together. We had almost everything: boats, motors, generators, a tractor, tools and the educational materials. We had everything but the needed truck. The only 4x4 truck to be found was the truck we had for the Mexico work. It was given years ago by a couple in Washington State. If we sent that truck, we would be without our only Mexico vehicle. Another problem was that the Venezuelan law did not permit the importation of a used truck.

Our Venezuelan friends and churches supporting them would trust God for the impossible provision of the importation, customs, taxes and port fees. We would trust Him for the impossible provision of the supplies and shipping to Venezuela. We all had hoped to get an exception from the Venezuelan government. They had an individual in high places in the government working to obtain a special exception, but this individual was transferred after the shipment was on its way and with this, our hopes were dashed.

Volunteers worked all day and late into the night to load the 40' shipping container parked in our

San Diego church parking lot. The morning the shipping company was to come, Eunie and I called Venezuela. Everything was loaded with just the exact space to fit in the truck. "Should we put it in, risking the truck and shipment?" we asked our friends. We all felt strongly that the truck should go. After hanging up the phone and looking at the clock—there was no more time. I'll never be known as a man of great faith. I felt very sure they should have the truck but very unsure about taking the risk and being responsible to all our partners for it. We prayed and went up to load the truck. After tying it down, we shut the doors and attached the shipping seals. The trucking company arrived shortly after and off went the shipping container, truck and all.

Weeks later I joined this missionary couple in Venezuela; Eunie stayed back to attend to work in Mexico. Of so many crazy events that took place in those next three weeks, many have to be left out here. Needless to say, we did everything possible to get our container out of the port. My frustrations and lack of faith are also best left out of the story!

The container arrived at the Venezuela port, but there was no way it could clear customs. We did everything possible--and impossible--to no avail. We even had a Christian captain in the National Guard taking us where no civilians could go to plead our case. We went to top Army, Navy and National Guard trying to find someone who could pry things open for us.

While we pled our case before the port authority, customs agents and the military controlling the port, we had fees and fines piling up against the value of the shipment.

Even without the problem of the truck, there was no way any of us could pay the taxes, fees and fines for the weeks we were stuck in the port; and every day, they were adding up. Every time I wrestle with "faith issues," God always seems to send someone to prod me. There was an elderly lady adding to my misery there. Every time I saw her, she would remind me that I needed to have more faith. That was easy for her to say.

Things went from impossibly bad to impossibly worse. One day our captain friend said the shipment was not going to be released. Our only chance was to talk to the President himself. I didn't like the plan. We would go to the Presidential Palace and the captain would go inside and through the military channels find out where we could intercept the President. Once past all the security, I was elected to petition the President. I think I felt at least as unprepared as Moses.

We went to the designated place and shortly after, armed security and military appeared everywhere. A presidential representative approached us and we explained our need to speak to the President. The representative passed us on to a general waiting for the President. The general said he would take care of us, made a call on his cell phone and sent us on our way to a colonel. The colonel was nice, but told us he couldn't help. What we wanted was impossible.

He personally sent us to the top man in their Internal Revenue Service and Customs for a closing hour appointment. We raced across the city and arrived to be escorted into a luxurious conference room. We were dirty, sweating and didn't smell so great after two days of running all over the city. After our meeting, this man gave me his card on which he wrote a note directing the head of the port to tend to our case. He then said to me, "You are in good hands." We left the office with his card, hurrying to arrive at the port authority's office by morning.

The next morning our confidence was dashed on the rocks as the port head told us it was illegal to do what was requested. We were now out of money and out of hope. If God didn't do a miracle the very next day, the container would be lost. Nothing had gone right. I wasn't feeling like much of a missionary.

The last day came, the day we had to accept our defeat. We were sitting in the custom agent's office when a fax from the capital came in for us. Big deal, it was the waiver of some tax. Too little, too late I thought. A little while later, another fax came waiving the other taxes. Then an envelope with some fancy government seal arrived on the port head's desk containing an official order for the truck to pass customs. Well that had to be God working! So although we still faced major fines and port fees, what followed could only be a miracle.

We took off running from one office to another, both exhausted and excited. Although we now owed big money to five different agencies, each agency waived our fees or fines. It was impossible but happened any way and all on the last day, at the last possible hour.

It was late Friday and the port was closing for the weekend. We couldn't find a truck anywhere that was big enough to move our container. The customs agent finally found a truck for us, but it was literally falling apart. We quickly contracted the driver and went into the port. Again we were denied access to the container.

The truck driver was angry. This time I was sure we were indeed "in good hands" and told him, "Don't worry. Watch, you are about to see a miracle." Even I—with my limited faith—was sure God was doing something. I won't forget the driver's bewildered expression as we were loaded and let out the guarded gates against all the normal rules and regulations. I sat on a bucket between the driver and my missionary friend. As we roared down the road out of the port city, we passed a statue of some lucky Catholic patron saint of the highway. The driver honked his horn, made the sign of the cross and kissed some religious thing he had. He should have done more.

About midnight, the truck's electrical system burned up. Driving through the dangerous mountains with the worn brakes was suddenly complicated by the fact that we couldn't see. We pulled off the narrow road and hung our hammocks under the truck. The mosquitoes quickly found us and so the prospects of sleep faded as the buzzing of the mosquitoes increased. We tried sleeping for a few hours, then gave up. We took down our hammocks and another big rig gave us a pull start with a chain.

We continued slowly by moonlight. A few hours before arriving at our destination, we found that the trees bordering the highway with their big extended limbs were too low for us to pass under. The driver figured that if we went fast enough, we could just break the limbs off. So we went, leaving limbs scattered all over the highway. The noise of smashing into the trees was horrendous.

We arrived after fourteen hours on the road and unloaded God's provision for God's people in God's time and in His way. As always, God didn't consult with me as to how I would have done it. The old Christian lady in the town just laughed at me, pointed her finger at me in joy and reminded me, "You just need to believe; you need to have faith." Easy for you to say, I thought again, but this time I was just glad to agree with her.

God does miracles with "stuff" from time to time. It encourages us since so much of life is related to "stuff," but of all things, these are the least important. As great as these things can seem to us, greater are the miracles He wants to do in us. Yes, we all like to see big things happen, but far more valuable are those little things He does in our lives. God wants us to not only remember that

He is able, but that we are unable. Oh yes, and we need to, like my old lady friend says with such a confident smile, "Have more faith. You just need to believe!"

The last truck available!

33

Reflections from the Amazon

Missionaries, just like anybody else, learn lessons from those who surround them. Those who surround us in life add perspective, challenge and flavor to our lives.

In early 2001 I was in Venezuela and traveled back upriver to the distant villages and Indians I have known over the years.

After long hours on the river under the hot sun, on the second day of our boat travel, we neared the falls. I guided the boat through the turbulent currents to the base of the falls. My Indian friend and I unloaded the remainder of 50 gallons of fuel, the outboard motor, the medicines and our supplies. We carried them to the top of the falls before dragging the small boat around the rocks to the top. Late that afternoon, we arrived at a village but it was empty. We later found all the people up a small stream in the jungle.

The people were going through a difficult time, daily searching the jungle for anything to eat. Their bananas, roots and other things they planted were still a long time from bearing.

Upon our arrival, we found a number of sick in need of medical attention. One woman was very close to death. Even with immediate care, we thought she would surely die that night. We went to her hammock in the middle of the night, while the witch doctor frantically worked to expel the cause of her sickness. I took her temperature—

105 degrees. After more medicine and bathing her with cool water, she fell asleep, her shallow breathing just a whisper.

Everyone in the small jungle camp was a bit calmer the next night. The Indian woman wasn't much better, but the medicine had begun to reverse her condition. That night, my friend talked late into the night as the people listened, slowly swinging in their hammocks with the small fires glowing throughout the camp. Although a lot of the language has escaped me over these last years, when he began telling the people about us foreigners, I grabbed my notebook and by the light of the fire began to record his words. You see, this Indian brother has been out of the jungle on an occasion and he observed us foreigners in detail and with curiosity.

His observations were many. Some were humorous. One, however, served as a lesson for me that night. He told these primitive people some things impossible for them to comprehend. He said the small plane they have sometimes seen flying high above their jungle is just a baby. The foreigners have big planes, really big planes. They are so big you have to climb up a ladder to get inside. He named four different villages known by the people and said they could all fit into the plane and it "would still be empty," something impossible for them to imagine.

As he continued I listened to the people comment and exclaim their amazement at all that was being said. He told them of "machines" the foreigners have that are like the boat in which we came, that go fast but on the ground (automobiles). This was impossible for them to imagine. He amazed them more when he told them that these machines have two flashlights like the one the foreigner has, referring to mine. "They go real fast in the dark with their flashlights. All the foreigners have them. If one foreigner gets too close to another foreigner, he will make a loud noise, 'honk, honk' to tell the other foreigner that he is mad and to get away from his machine."

He told them he had seen all these things himself and had even been in one of those running machines. All this stimulated a lot of conversation among the others who loudly exclaimed their amazement and fear about the jungle of the foreigners. There were other things he told about us and our culture which were interesting to hear from his perspective; the last, however, was more sobering than entertaining.

His comment brought exclamations of amazement from the people but stirred in me sadness. He continued, "The foreigners never get hungry. Everywhere the foreigners go there is food and they are always eating. There is lots of food in their jungle and they are always eating. They are never hungry."

With that, there were more exclamations of astonishment and these from a people who basically live with hunger. They have no concept in their world and culture of just how much we have, neither would they be able to comprehend the common statement voiced daily across our "jungle" (land), "Just throw it out; I can't eat anymore. I'm full."

When we become accustomed to certain blessings, we tend to forget to be appreciative and thankful. We can even adopt the attitude that these things are our right to have, use and even waste and we deserve what we want in abundance. This is beyond the imagination of much of the rest of the world.

Gratitude is a powerful disposition. It makes us a bit more humble and appreciative. It may even lead to our being more like wise stewards as opposed to feeling that we deserve so much. It could challenge us to live a little more simply. Gratitude is also the highest and purest motive and motivation of any real ministry, although apparently in short supply with many popular ministries today. It's great to have abundance, but greater still is to realize that it's only a stewardship. How life changes when we are sincerely grateful for even the small things.

I couldn't help think, "How would we live our Christian lives if only every once in a while we were even half as amazed as my Indian friends as to how blessed we really are? How can that realization increase my gratitude today and challenge my Christian living to a higher level?"

The fires burned down and everyone drifted off to sleep in the darkness. The jungle frogs, birds, animals and distant thunder and rain drowned out the last commentaries; I, however, had to think a bit longer.

Years prior to this I was impressed by another lesson learned in company of Indian friends and a friend from the USA who accompanied me.

We were traveling by dugout canoe, on three rivers concluding with a long journey up a narrow stream to a village where we were to work. Although the water was very low, we navigated the three rivers without any problem. But starting up the narrow stream was a different story. The low water uncovered countless trees which had fallen across the stream. Normally covered by deep water, the low water revealed our many obstacles.

As I navigated the outboard motor around rocks, big limbs and fallen trees, the alligators and big stingrays in the shallow water scattered. If a fallen tree lay partially submerged, we would go towards it at full speed and jump the canoe over it. At the last second, we would cut the power and lift the foot of the motor quickly out of the water to avoid hitting the tree. Although we "jumped" many trees, there were others we had to cut through.

By the end of the first day, all of us had broken open blisters from our many turns with the ax. We had not brought any food with us because we had anticipated our arrival in the village before sunset. When it was too dark to go on, we made camp. Each of us hung up our hammock and went to sleep exhausted.

The next morning we got up early and continued. It was late in the day and all of us were all the more exhausted, our hands were all torn up and we were very hungry. I was standing in the back of the canoe driving the outboard motor.

As we rounded one tight turn in the stream, all of a sudden the Indian in front of the canoe started to wave his arms. I turned off the motor, and soon we were drifting back. What was out of my sight was what the Indian in the front of our long canoe was all excited about--dinner.

I only got a glimpse of it as we floated back. It looked like a giant tire thrown up on the bank. A big snake! The canoe came to a sudden stop as the back, where I was standing, hit up against the bank. Everyone was excited. We would eat tonight!

I should have been a little more doubtful. It seemed a little convenient to hand the shot gun to me since I just happened to be the one closest to step out of the canoe. As I stood there with the shot gun, everyone's affirmative expression and gestures didn't seem to provoke any boldness within me. The quick-witted Indian who was sitting in front of me saw that I wasn't that excited about climbing up the bank to face the snake by myself. So he stood up and said, "Let's go."

I figured if he wasn't too worried about it, I wasn't going to worry either. As we started up the bank, he whispered, "Certainly shoot him in the head."

When we got to the top of the bank, all of a sudden I didn't feel so hungry anymore. Just five feet in front of us was a giant, sleeping anaconda.

My buddy was right behind me, encouraging me on. I raised the shot gun and quietly stepped up to the side of the anaconda. Extending the gun towards his head, my anxiety subsided momentarily as I pulled the trigger. However, it did not produce the expected "bang," but rather a very unsettling "click." Following the "click" was a feeling of being in a terrible nightmare movie. It didn't seem possible. I suddenly felt so powerless.

Sometimes the shot gun shells don't fire the first time. I quickly pulled back the hammer again, aimed and to my disbelief, got another "click" instead of "bang."

Before I could worry about the shell not firing a second time, the anaconda awoke. That big head turned towards me and in a flash of a second lunged up into my face. I guess there are advantages to being ugly. Somehow I must have been uglier to the anaconda than he was to me, because after getting in my face, it lunged off to the side and down the bank towards the canoe. I just stood there watching the coils of the giant snake unwind as it flung itself into the river.

I turned around in disbelief to see the expression of my Indian friend, but he was not behind me. As soon as I had pulled up the shot gun at the anaconda, he had left me and had run back to the canoe. I climbed back down the bank. Everyone was too startled to speak, sitting and looking at each other. They had heard nothing when unexpectedly, above their heads, was a flying anaconda. It hit the bank and had gone under the canoe.

The failed shotgun shell reminded me of how often we rest our faith on things working out one way or another. They don't always work out how we think they will or should. This can serve as a reminder of keeping our priorities and life values in line.

Although it would have been nice to have had dinner that night, it was greater still, going to hammock not having been dinner. Jeff Hummel, from Pennsylvania, was a great encouragement to everyone on that trip and took everything in stride, including the "flying anaconda" which descended from the high bank upon him and the Indians.

Apart from the work we went to do there, brother Hummel raised funds before our trip to obtain malaria medication unavailable in Venezuela. Because of his efforts, lives were spared.

A new lesson at every turn! I started the motor, and we continued upriver. We arrived in the village late the following day.

34

Mistaken Ideas

During the late 1970's and early 1980's; I, like countless others, had a lot of mistaken ideas about missionaries and those who "support" them. It wasn't long after, however, that these ideas got a needed adjustment. While working with North, Central and South American groups, churches and missions; I've found that to varying degrees, mistaken ideas concerning missionary life and partners are quite prevalent. These mistaken ideas have become of concern to us because they tend to contribute to a number of harmful premises.

In the mid-1990's these concerns led us to write a two-part article which was published in the New Tribes Mission magazine, "Brown Gold."

-Part One-

Mistaken Ideas:
We are left with stereotypes of missions that need to be updated.

"This missionary was chased by a jaguar. He wrestled an alligator, killing it with his bare hands to have something with which to feed his family when they had run out of food. He was shot in the shoulder with a seven-foot arrow, when entering a village to teach the Word. On another journey to take God's Word to an unreached village, a 14-foot boa constrictor dropped from the thick jungle, wrapping itself around our missionary, almost killing him.

After walking five days through the jungle without food, he found himself in the middle of a tribal war, arrows flying by in both directions.

Meanwhile, his wife was washing clothes at the river's edge, and was attacked by piranha. She was bleeding badly from the brutal attack and, although in shock, was able to stitch up her own wounds with a needle and sewing thread."

With this introduction, the pastor of "First Church" presented the missionary family, back on furlough from South America. Standing by him was the husband, skinny, perhaps 120 pounds and about 5'6" tall; the frail wife greeted the church with a meek, almost inaudible voice.

The first words the missionary shared were, "We on the mission field are no different from anyone else. Our struggles are the same as your struggles. We battle with our flesh just as you do. No one needs a special call for missions; missions is for ordinary folks...."

The eyes of the congregation were as big as truck-stop pancakes. A math teacher, with a family of five, was sitting in the front row thinking to himself, "Ordinary folks! These people seem far from ordinary to me. What does he mean, no special call needed? Getting arrows shot at me, being attacked by tigers and giant snakes and killing wild beasts just to have breakfast is not my idea of a career. To live like that, I would need a very, very special call from God."

Although the face of world missions has changed much in the past decade, and is changing at an ever-increasing pace, many of us still look upon missionaries as a special breed from another era. Is it any wonder many hold to the idea that missionaries are different, not so ordinary, even a bit strange, and are suspicious of the claim made that they had no special call to live such wild lives?

The real truth is that circumstances, lifestyles and living situations vary as much on the mission field as they do at home. We are, however, left with stereotypes of missions that need to be updated. What many missionaries have been trying to communicate to our churches is not so much the idea that life in other lands is comparable to theirs, and that the life challenges one faces are similar. Often, they are not. However, when a missionary says that their lives out there on the mission field are no different than ours here, he may be addressing a more internal issue not so easily explained, yet ironically, one with which we can easily identify.

Here it is: Life out there may indeed be different, but its focus is on that which reflects a change God brings about within us, captivating the inner man, lighting fire to a desire to walk with Jesus, to take His Word to the lost, even going to faraway lands to share His Words of life. This is the life fire meant for *all* believers.

We all need to be challenged--our faith needs to be challenged--yet it is God who will best give the geographic direction. Of first importance is *who we are, not where we go.* So, whether you feel or don't feel like an anxious volunteer for missions, the real root of the matter is walking "in Jesus," not so much "after Him." When it comes to interest in missions, we should hope to be better Christians than missionaries. A good missionary might get sent home!

Look with me at Mark 5. A demon-possessed man was set free by Jesus. This man lived in darkness, enslaved by the Enemy who sought to destroy him physically and spiritually. This man fell in love with Jesus and was immediately ready to do anything for Him and even sought to go with Jesus to other villages. Yet this missionary was sent home!

"And as He was getting into the boat, the man who had been demon-possessed was entreating Him that he might accompany Him. And He did not let him, but He said to him, "Go home to your people and report to them what great things the Lord has done for you and how He had mercy on you. And he went away and began to proclaim in Decapolis what great things Jesus had done for him; and everyone marveled."   (Mark 5:18-20)

If one thing is lacking above all else in our churches, and even on our mission fields, it is our lost gratitude and thanksgiving which give life to all testimony, and compel many to come to Jesus asking, "Where would you use me, Lord?"

In closing, the mission field is really the same as our homeland in some ways. In both places, "good missionaries" are needed. So whether you have signed up to go or God has kept you back, locale is of secondary importance.

After all, perhaps you may not do well at killing alligators and running from tigers and snakes (but please pray for those who do!). Overseas missions have changed a lot, but the fire that drives it has not. This fire needs to be rekindled.

"And he went away and began to proclaim in Decapolis what great things Jesus had done for him; and everyone marveled."   (Mark 5:20)

- Part Two -

Mistaken Ideas
How can missions fit into an average guys' life?

He wakes up early and leaves his dwelling before his children awake. He fights through busy traffic and may keep a next-to-impossible schedule. With his bare hands he must accomplish incredible tasks to earn an income to feed his family. He lives and works in an environment often characterized by immoral and offensive gestures or talk. He must wrestle with deadlines, quotas and demands as part of his daily life to provide for his family and, alas--through his sacrificial giving--make it possible for missionary efforts to go forth to reach lost tribes with the Gospel of Jesus Christ! Yes, this is the heroic individual who is commonly referred to as "a supporter."

Traditional ideas have left us with some funny perceptions of foreign missionaries, yet they are not the only ones carrying a mistaken stereotype. It's been said, "If you can't go to the mission field, you can *at least* give so that someone else can go." That sounds like an assigning of secondary importance to me. Is it possible that there is a stereotyping of those who may not necessarily be gifted for overseas service? There may be some mistaken ideas reflected about the role of the home partner?

Have you ever been left feeling you are only as good as the level of your financial support when it comes to missions? There is a lot more to your importance than your wallet! May I remind you that although not every believer is meant to live a "missionary lifestyle," every believer is meant to live a "Christian lifestyle." A believer in Jesus' day wanted to follow Him, yet Jesus gave him another important task: *"Go home and be a witness."* (Mark 5:18-20).

We must not make the mistake of viewing our participation or calling as exclusively geographical or task-oriented in scope. It is much more important who we are in Christ than where we live or what we do. In today's missions, we need some constructive rethinking on both the foreign field as well as at home. Mistaken ideas prevail.

So, you may be one of those God has chosen to use at home, but you have the desire to be a part of what God is doing in reaching the lost overseas.

But how can missions fit into an average guy's life?

After all, between work, traveling to and from work, attending church twice a week, and trying to balance family and some community ministry, there isn't really a lot of time left. And after going shopping to put food on the table, paying of rent or mortgage and other bills, there may not be a whole lot of cash left. "What can I or my family do to join in seeing the lost reached?" you might ask.

I would like to offer the following suggestions to you who want to do more concerning missions, but have limited time and/or finances.

1. Consider yourself involved in a partnership. If you pray or give to a missionary somewhat regularly, I would not consider you a supporter, but a partner.

2. Although partnership requires each participant to perform certain tasks, remember that the individual on the field can not do his part if we at home do not do ours. The man at home is equally important!

3. Whether on the field or at home, each of us as Christians needs to evaluate priorities and "needs." We can all make adjustments in lifestyle and living standards for the building of the Kingdom.

4. Don't just pray for a missionary, ask him to pray for you too. Missionaries aren't the only ones who need prayer. Don't think they are too busy. They can't afford to be too busy to pray for you, just as you can make time to pray for them.

5. Swap two or three personal prayer requests with your missionary partner. Be specific, be personal and ask your missionary to do the same.

6. Take that time you spend on the road going to work or shopping to really get down to praying for your missionary partner. Even if you only travel five or ten minutes, that time in prayer is much more than many Christians spend at home praying.

7. Break that stereotype of being "a missions supporter" sitting down once a month and writing a support check. That's not what it's all about. What a mistaken idea! You're a vital member of a very important partnership.

35
Puzzle Pieces

Although God has allowed me the privilege of serving in the jungle and in a number of countries, the place I have spent the majority of my ministry has been, up to today, in Mexico. The years of work leading to the day on which I write this page have been filled with both joyful and bitter experiences, violence and freedom, great fellowship and deep loneliness. Some things are difficult to describe; others are best not mentioned.

In the beginning of this small book I said, "The following story is not one reflecting the events and changes or accomplishments of any number of men, but rather a collection of events reflecting an onward moving process of the Spirit of God, being hindered by sin."

Each of our lives is like a puzzle, slowly being put together. Puzzle pieces, each playing a part in life's drama; some bigger, some smaller. It's been more than two decades since I started writing what would become this book. I am painfully aware of a greater number of shortcomings in my life, more now than ten or fifteen years back. In my life, I hope each puzzle piece leaves me reflecting more on God's person, love and grace. Even in this hope, I know I fall short. In completing these final pages, I look back over their content. I have shared some personal things which I trust, hope and pray will encourage and be in some way of help to those considering them.

I don't so much believe that people are at different places in their spiritual growth but rather that we all are simply growing spiritually in different places in life. God wants to fit our lives together in a way only He can in a world so full of disappointment, pain, tragedy and vanity which affect us all. Some of us, who are very busy with many things, including "Christian things," may find that it's been all too long since we gave much attention to how our life's "puzzle" is coming together. We may find it difficult to "balance" out the different pieces of life as we journey through its seasons. Even so, each of us possesses the power to determine how much of our attention will be given to the working out of our faith through the fabric of life.

The only real difference among Christians is that some live out their faith while others don't even think much about it. While some seek to conform their lives to God's Word, others try to accommodate God's Word to their own lives and values. Each one decides how he or she will build upon that foundation which is Christ (1 Corinthians 3:10-15).

Are you, my friend, having a difficult time getting the pieces in the right places? May these pages challenge and encourage you. If you are struggling, you are not alone. Fight the good fight, finish the course, keep the faith; God is fitting your life together. Are you someone who has struggled to see how you fit into the "big picture" or wrestled with reconciling your faith to the rest of life? Or do you feel that there must be more to your "Christianity," but you just can't seem to find it or embrace it? It's there; don't get discouraged, friend. Keep seeking; you may be closer than you think. Each puzzle piece has its place.

Last year I was in Venezuela for a short time. For part of that time, I was able to travel back upriver to visit a group of Indians I have known over the years. I took with me an Indian friend I first met almost twenty-five years ago. I remember him as a committed believer then. I've seen how God has worked in and through his life since. His constant eternal perspective coupled with his unflinching concern for his people has greatly inspired me. There is much I could say about this man, his faith and his bold testimony. We have traveled together many times to distant villages.

Some years ago, we slowly traveled by night up a river and found a village on the river's edge. The people excitedly ran to the bank with torches to see who we were. They took us to their village for the night. Once in the village, a witch doctor came out and asked what we were doing there. He was very upset because his spirits had become afraid when we had arrived. He loudly mocked my partner and tried to turn the people against us.

I was tired from navigating the boat all day, so I hung my hammock and went right to sleep. Late that night, my partner overheard the people plotting to do us harm. Early in the morning, while it was still dark, he came and woke me. We quietly took down our hammocks and ducked out a small hole in the village wall and into the jungle, down to the canoe and sped off into the thick fog.

A couple of years later, he wanted to return to talk to the people there. We returned up that river to their trail. It was overgrown with vines, so we cut our way through and found an empty village peppered with burned spots on the ground. Almost all the people had died in a malaria epidemic and were burned by the few who had survived. As we quietly walked around the village, I saw the deep sadness in the eyes of this man who had hoped to help them.

Although he is a bit older now (I guess I am too!), he is still strongly walking God's trail. Last year, while on our way back from visiting the people upriver, we pulled the boat over and stopped for the night. We cut out an area to make camp and then hung our hammocks. After gathering firewood and getting a fire going, we sat in our hammocks and began to talk. I asked him about different people from over the years. He spoke with great sadness of those who had heard God's Word but were not following God's trail. He talked for a good while.

As he spoke, he seemed most moved in remembering those who had thrown away God's talk to walk other trails, trails that have led to much hurt and sadness. He paused for a moment, staring at the ground and then leaped to his feet next to the fire slapping his chest. With overwhelming conviction, he raised his voice, "But I will never throw Him away! Jesus Christ is mine! He is mine and I'll never throw the Great Spirit away! He is the only trail!" I guess it doesn't come out that clearly in English, but you get the point.

Searching through the meaning, purpose and sum total of all of life's pursuits, have you come to this same overwhelming conviction? Can you say with our friend in the Amazon, "Yes, He is the only trail; He is my only trail"?

When Jesus called individuals after Himself, to follow Him, they walked with Him, not so much after Him. We would do well to draw a bit closer to the Lord, to not be so given to the insignificant values and pursuits of this life at the expense of the greater things.

"Greater things" come into clearer focus when seen alongside the other pursuits of life that oppose them. What are these "greater things"?

Love the Lord your God
with all your heart
and with all your soul
and with all your mind
and with all your strength...

and love your neighbor as yourself.
There is no commandment greater than these.

So, de vez en cuando, from time to time, take some time to look back, reflect, re-evaluate. Life's short span should not allow for many such stops, yet, from time to time, take time to look back, remember, meditate and consider.

Reflect on the faces, experiences, places and events which have formed and altered your being, your values, your perspective and your purposes in life. Take time to thank God for who and what you are in Him, for what you have and, if possible, even for your pains, your losses and your disappointments. Life is short. Make the best of it for eternity. Keep your eyes on Jesus, the author and perfector of your faith.

The time is now; tomorrow may not be. Jesus stands before us, before a great multitude and calls again...

About the Author

Rick Johnson is the founder and director of International Action Ministries. He, together with his wife, Eunice, continue to minister in villages and settlements like those mentioned in this book.

Their work allows others to form partnerships with them and the nationals participating with their ministry. Ministry is multiplying through teaching and discipling others to walk with the Savior, obeying all things that He has commanded.

All proceeds from this publication go to further the work of International Action Ministries in nurturing new outreach and in doing so, seeing those who are the focus of today's ministry become tomorrow's ministers.

For more information on how you can be involved contact:

Rick and Eunice Johnson
International Action Ministries
2610 Galveston Street
San Diego, California 92110